1978

NATHANIEL HAWTHORNE

The Poetics of Enchantment

Also by Edgar A. Dryden
Melville's Thematics of Form

NATHANIEL HAWTHORNE
The Poetics of Enchantment

EDGAR A. DRYDEN

Cornell University Press ITHACA AND LONDON

First published 1977 by Cornell University Press.
Published in the United Kingdom by Cornell University Press Ltd., 2–4 Brook Street, London W1Y 1AA.

International Standard Book Number 0–8014–1028–2
Library of Congress Catalog Card Number 76-28010
Printed in the United States by York Composition Co., Inc.
Librarians: Library of Congress cataloging information appears on the last page of the book.

For my parents

Contents

Preface

> Criticism is the mimetic duplication of a conceptual action.
> . . . To experience anew in one's own mind the *cogito* of a
> writer or a philosopher means to rediscover the manner of
> thinking and feeling, means to see how this thinking and
> feeling originate and assume form and what obstacles they
> encounter. It means also to rediscover the purpose of a life
> which takes shape out of the experience of the individual
> consciousness.
>
> Georges Poulet, "Poulet on Poulet: The Self
> and the Other in Critical Consciousness"

Who is Nathaniel Hawthorne? This question puzzled
Hawthorne's contemporaries—even his family and friends—
has perplexed his biographers and critics, and continues to
be asked by students who read his work. The most common
complaint of my undergraduate students of Hawthorne is
that he deliberately obscures his own relation to his work
and to his reader. Unlike Melville, they argue, who seems to
live in and through *Moby-Dick*, Hawthorne appears deliberately to dissociate his personal existence from the intricate patterns and balanced sentences of *The Scarlet Letter*
while, at the same time, seeming to insist on the priority
of the personal. Why is it, a student once asked me during a
discussion of *The Scarlet Letter*, that Hawthorne introduces his book with such a long discussion of himself and
his problems when the book itself seems completely unre-

lated to the history, biography, or psychology of Nathaniel Hawthorne?

The last twenty years of Hawthorne scholarship make clear that there are a number of ways one could try to answer such a question. The symbolic readings of Roy Male, Richard Fogle, Hyatt Waggoner, and others, the psychoanalytic perspective of Frederick Crews, the psycho-poetic approach of Jean Normand: all are in one way or another attempts to describe the form of Hawthorne's presence in his work, to connect the biographical and literary selves. This is, of course, a familiar problem in literary studies in general and may be especially central to the study of fiction. Novelists traditionally have been preoccupied with the issues of pseudonymity and anonymity, with the relationship between their real and fictive selves.[1] From Cervantes through Defoe and Richardson, three writers who were important to Hawthorne, concern with the nature of the writer's identity is so central that it becomes more a thematic than simply a biographical or psychological issue. So too with Hawthorne. For him the relation between a writer's personal identity and its manifestation to the world is a part of the larger problem of the relation between man's inner and social beings. Writing for Hawthorne is the expression of a particular way of being related to the world,

---

[1] For three especially perceptive discussions of this problem see Jean Starobinski, "Truth in Masquerade," in *Stendhal: A Collection of Critical Essays,* ed. Victor Brombert (Englewood Cliffs: Prentice-Hall, 1962), pp. 114–126; Leo Bersani, *Balzac to Beckett: Center and Circumference in French Fiction* (New York: Oxford University Press, 1970), pp. 3–23; Homer O. Brown, "The Displaced Self in the Novels of Daniel Defoe," *English Literary History,* 38 (December 1971), pp. 562–590.

and, for this reason, the writer's self may best be thought of as a thematic self, a self that may be defined simply as the organizing principle or conceptual center of his work.

To suggest that the writer's self is his major theme, however, is not to imply that he is immediately available to his reader. Like a name, the surface of a text may conceal as much as it expresses. Hawthorne, more than most writers perhaps, is fascinated by the ways in which a writer's work is at once a disguise he wears and a manifestation of his most intimate concerns. The writer, he reminds us, cannot be known through the study of any one character, story, or novel. The reader who hopes to know him intimately must "look through the whole range of his fictitious characters."[2] Following his advice, I have approached his work as a totality —setting his stories, sketches, novels, nonfictional writings (including letters) together—and have sought within it for those repeated obsessions and attitudes that provide its underlying structures and organizing principles, for these are the clues to the writer's relation to himself and to others. I have not, therefore, attempted to provide full interpretations of individual stories and novels. Many admirable interpretations of individual works already exist, and my primary concern has been to uncover the similarities among all the works and to identify the unvarying patterns throughout Hawthorne's career as a writer.

This strategy is consistent with another of his basic assumptions, namely, that a writer's development often takes the form of a gradual coming-to-awareness of the hidden truths that have been central to his work from the begin-

[2] *The Complete Works of Nathaniel Hawthorne* (Cambridge, 1882), III, 386.

ning. "In youth, men are apt to write more wisely than they really know or feel; and the remainder of life may be not idly spent in realizing and convincing themselves of the wisdom which they uttered long ago. The truth that was only in the fancy then may have since become a substance in the mind and heart."[3] Although this observation provides another reason for viewing a writer's work as a totality, it also suggests that the later work may be especially illuminating, since one would expect to find there the writer's original impulses or basic themes in their most obvious and most tangible form. Moreover, the statement associates the writer's development with a process so basic in Hawthorne's world that it appears at every level of his experience. The transformation of the shadows of fancy into the substances of the mind and heart is an incarnation, and that process in Hawthorne's world always disenchants and demystifies. Consequently, my final chapter, which traces the theme of homelessness in his work, focuses on *The Marble Faun* and the unfinished romances, texts that signal the end of enchantment and mark the conclusion of Hawthorne's career as a novelist.

The themes of enchantment and disenchantment, then, are central. An alternating movement between enchanted realms and the cold hillside is the dominating force in Hawthorne's work, determining the form of his characters' relations to one another, of the narrators' relations to their characters, and finally, of the novelist's relation not only to his narrators and characters but to the reader as well. For Hawthorne's exploration of enchanted ground focuses not

[3] Ibid., p. 388.

on the relation between self and nature but on the relation between self and others. Two themes persist throughout the body of his writings and shape and control its form and development: enchantment and disenchantment—enchantment as the condition generated by the lure of others and disenchantment as the discovery that the lure is deceptive and dangerous, that the experience of the other is at best fugitive and tenuous, at worst alienating and threatening. These themes have a number of versions, and I examine several of the more prominent ones in the following chapters. The problem of solitude, the themes of love and wandering, the question of the relation between writer and reader: these are all variants of that basic pattern and are connected in complicated and interesting ways. I have attempted first to unravel the form of their interconnection and second to suggest the ways in which each is related to that unity we call Nathaniel Hawthorne.

My approach to Hawthorne, then, takes the form of an inside narrative. Such an approach necessarily differs from those that place the critic outside the text and regard his role as one of investigation and then measurement of results against those of other investigators. From my perspective (and from Hawthorne's) literary fictions do not appear as things fixed and unchanging that can be surveyed and described dispassionately and objectively. The expressions we habitually use to describe our experiences with such texts sufficiently show their uniqueness. When we speak of being "caught up by a book," of "losing ourselves in it," of being "overwhelmed by it," "enveloped by it," we are identifying a spell cast over us by the fictive world, an enchantment as mystifying as the games of childhood; and as long as we breathe the hallucinating atmosphere of this world, which is after all no more than black marks on a page, we lose our sense of our own identities and give ourselves over to a realm that does not exist. The pleasure we derive from this experience causes us to wish that the book would never end and produces in us that disappointment we always feel on turning the final page of a novel. For if fictions resemble the games of childhood, they recall too those experiences most often associated with the loss of childhood innocence. While some fictions are longer than others (dedicated readers usually prefer the longer ones), all must end sooner or later and with that end comes disenchantment in the form of a sense of loss.

Criticism begins here and seeks to recover and order the experience of reading. Hence if I have made a few references to the works of other scholars and critics it has been in order to focus more directly on my own experience of Hawthorne. I wish, however, to acknowledge my debt to other students of Hawthorne who share my enthusiasm for his writings and to emphasize that my reading is not offered in opposition to theirs. Although some readings are more convincing than others, most readings both illuminate and veil, for to emphasize one aspect of a text is to slight others. I offer this reading in the hope that it will illuminate a side of Hawthorne which the more familiar symbolic and psychoanalytic approaches have left veiled, and in so doing that it will supplement rather than counter the readings of others.

In preparing this study I have incurred a number of debts I am glad to acknowledge here. First, I want to thank friends and colleagues at Buffalo who read and commented on portions of the manuscript: Richard Fly, Roy Roussel, Murray Schwartz, and Fred See. I am also grateful for the assistance and encouragement of Homer Brown and Joseph Riddel, good friends and exemplary readers.

Earlier versions of parts of this study have already been published. Some paragraphs appeared in "Hawthorne's Castle in the Air: Form and Theme in *The House of the Seven Gables*," *English Literary History*, 38 (June 1971), 294–317, © 1971 The Johns Hopkins University Press; grateful acknowledgment is made to Arnold Stein, senior editor, and to The Johns Hopkins University Press. Other sections first appeared in "The Limits of Romance: A Reading of *The Marble Faun*," in *Individual and Community*, eds. Kenneth H. Baldwin and David K. Kirby (Durham: Duke University Press, 1975), pp. 17–48, and are reprinted here by permission of Duke University Press.

Finally, I am indebted to the Research Foundation of the State of New York for two Summer Fellowships, which provided necessary research time.

EDGAR A. DRYDEN

Buffalo, New York

A Note on Texts

I have used the available volumes of *The Centenary Edition of the Works of Nathaniel Hawthorne*, eds. William Charvat, Roy Harvey Pearce, and Claude Simpson (Columbus: Ohio State University Press, 1962–). For those texts not yet published in the Ohio State edition I have used *The Complete Works of Nathaniel Hawthorne*, 12 vols. (Cambridge: Houghton Mifflin, 1882), except where there are more reliable or complete texts in other editions. For convenience I have used the following abbreviations.

CE   *The Centenary Edition of the Works of Nathaniel Hawthorne*, eds. William Charvat, Roy Harvey Pearce, and Claude Simpson. Columbus: Ohio State University Press, 1962–).

CW   *The Complete Works of Nathaniel Hawthorne*, 12 vols. Cambridge: Houghton Mifflin, 1882.

DGS   *Hawthorne's Doctor Grimshaw's Secret*, ed. Edward H. Davidson. Cambridge: Harvard University Press, 1954.

EN   *The English Notebooks*, ed. Randall Stewart. New York: Modern Language Association, 1941; reprinted, New York: Russell & Russell, 1962.

LL   *The Love Letters of Nathaniel Hawthorne 1839–1863*, 2 vols. Chicago: The Society of the Dofobs, 1907; reprinted in one volume, with Foreword by C. E. Frazer Clark, Washington: NCR/Microcard Editions, 1972.

1

The Enchantment of Distance

Lights and shadows are continually flitting across my inward sky, and I know neither whence they come nor whither they go; nor do I inquire too closely into them. It is dangerous to look too minutely at such phenomena. It is apt to create a substance, where at first there was a mere shadow.

Love Letters of Nathaniel Hawthorne, 1839–1863

Hawthorne's spiritual adventure begins in a refusal to withdraw into his own being, with a conscious decision to ignore the shadowy presences that occupy his inner world. Nevertheless he is haunted by those presences that he fears to encounter and that are at once strange and at the center of his being. Indeed, so central are those haunting lights and shadows that Hawthorne's refusal to examine them takes on the dignity and importance of a genetic moment and makes the fear, of which his refusal is the sign, the hidden ground and foundation of everything else in his world. For Hawthorne, there is no pure moment of self-awareness when the mind separates from everything but itself. In his world human consciousness in finding itself finds not only itself but an other as well. Those unknown lights and shadows are not signs of pure selfhood but are the reflections of the other to which the self is inextricably bound. Hence Hawthorne's fear of inner exploration derives not so much from the dread that such a journey will seal him forever within himself and thereby prevent him from reaching out to others as it does from a conviction that such a voyage will lead to the discovery of a menacing otherness at his own center.

A preoccupation with one's inwardness, in other words, leads not to isolation but rather to the "horrible ugliness of . . . exposure" (*CE* I, 194). In Hawthorne's fiction those characters who are "rendered morbidly self-contemplative" (155) are also those characters who are most sensitive to the presence of others and, at the same time, are the ones most driven to open themselves to others. Those who, like Dimmesdale and Roderick Elliston, become "acutely conscious of a self" find that it becomes "so prominent an object with them, that they cannot but present it to the face of every casual passer-by" (*CE* X, 273). In spite of themselves they are driven by their "diseased self-contemplation" (283) to the "naked exposure of something that ought not to be left prominent" (*CE* III, 92) and hence to a violation of the "sacredness of the individual" (*LL* II, 62–63), the "sanctity of a human heart" (*CE* I, 195). Hawthorne's solitary introspective characters are haunted by dreams of such an exposure. Hepzibah Pyncheon fears that her brother Clifford will become a "figure such as one imagines himself to be, with the world's eye on him, in a troubled dream" (*CE* II, 247), and Dr. Dolliver, driven by the loneliness of old age into an unhealthy introspection, experiences a "nightmare-feeling which we sometimes have in dreams, when we seem to find ourselves wandering through a crowded avenue, with the noonday sun upon us, in some wild extravagance of dress or nudity" (*CW* XI, 32).

Hawthorne's distrust of the lights and shadows of his inner world derives from a similar fear of standing naked and defenseless before the probing eyes of an other. When he writes to Sophia in an attempt to excuse his reluctance to announce their engagement to his family, he stresses the importance of keeping his "inner and essential self" (*LL* II, 78) hidden from himself as well as from others.

I do not think thou canst estimate what a difficult task thou didst propose to me—not that any awful and tremendous effect would be produced by the disclosure; but because of the strange reserve, in regard to matters of feeling, that has always existed among us. We are conscious of one another's feelings, always; but there seems to be a tacit law, that our deepest heart-concernments are not to be spoken of. I cannot gush out in their presence—I cannot take my heart in my hand, and show it to them. There is a feeling within me . . . as if it would be as indecorous to do so, as to display to them the naked breast.

. . . . .

I tell thee these things, in order that my Dove, into whose infinite depths the sunshine falls continually, may perceive what a cloudy veil stretches over the abyss of my nature. Thou wilt not think that it is caprice or stubbornness that has made me hitherto resist thy wishes. Neither, I think, is it a love of secrecy and darkness. I am glad to think that God sees through my heart; and if any angel has power to penetrate into it, he is welcome to know everything that is there. Yes; and so may any mortal, who is capable of full sympathy, and therefore worthy to come into my depths. But he must find his own way there. I can neither guide him nor enlighten him. It is this in-voluntary reserve, I suppose, that has given the objectivity to my writings. And when people think that I am pouring myself out in a tale or essay, I am merely telling what is common to human nature, not what is peculiar to myself. I sympathise with them—not they with me. [*LL* II, 78–80]

As this admirable passage makes clear, an awareness of the other is at the center of Hawthorne's most intimate concerns. The other is present for him, however, in two very different ways. It is most painfully and poignantly revealed through the experience of shame. No writer before Sartre is more sensitive than Hawthorne to the ways the probing scrutiny of others in shaming us robs us of our autonomy and spontaneity. For him as for Sartre the fear of being surprised in a state of nakedness symbolizes man's vulnerability to the gaze of the other. The wearing of clothes, therefore, at once testifies to man's desire to see without being seen and allows him to relate to others in a mediated and superficial way.[1] As a symbol of the frontier separating the "I" from the rest of the world, clothes allow men to communicate without revealing their "deepest heart-concernments." In this way they resemble most of man's "customs and prejudices" (*CE* X, 280) which are an "instinctive effort" to keep hidden "beneath a heap of superficial topics, which constitute the materials of intercourse between man and man" (278) the disturbing truth that the other is an ontological dimension of the self.

Such mediating devices, however, are tenuous at best, since for Hawthorne one's own gaze is capable of initiating the degrading process of exposure. He associates the emotion of shame with self-discovery as well as with direct encounter with the other. Therefore, the "cloudy veil" that keeps his inner depths hidden from his own eyes is as important a garment as those concealing his nakedness from the world at large. Roderick Elliston's bosom serpent makes him an object of "curiosity and conjecture" (*CE* X, 271), but the snake is engendered by a "diseased self-contemplation" (283), not by the threatening gaze of others. By focusing directly on his inner shadows, Roderick transforms a "dark fantasy" into a "substance," and then pays "full allegiance to [the] humiliating law" (274) that compels him to expose himself to the eyes of the world. Only at last

[1] See Jean-Paul Sartre, *Being and Nothingness*, trans. Hazel E. Barnes (New York: Citadel Press, 1971), pp. 197–278. See also José Ortega y Gasset's discussion of the relationship between self-consciousness and shame in *What Is Philosophy?*, trans. Mildred Adams (New York: Norton, 1960), pp. 177–181.

when he heeds his wife's advice to "forget yourself in the idea of another" does the process reverse itself and the serpent become again a "dark fantasy and what it typified . . . as shadowy as itself" (283).

Avoiding Roderick's problem (the transformation of inner shadows into a threatening substance), however, is not as easy as "The Bosom Serpent" and the "inward sky" passage (this chapter's epigraph) suggest. It is true that Hawthorne's characters are free to turn their eyes away from their inner shadows and to give priority to those faculties directing the mind outward to the world. But just as Roderick's self-contemplation begets otherness so concentration on the other leads back to self. The generating force of this movement, however, is sympathy rather than shame, and the other is perceived as the source of life rather than as some death-dealing gorgon. In this situation men experience themselves as united to nature and to other men by reciprocal waves of sympathy. At these moments of union they feel themselves not only a part of the "surging stream of human sympathy" (*CE* II, 165), mankind's "warm and sympathetic life" (*CW* XI, 287), but "in sympathy with nature as well, in brotherhood with all that [breathes] around them" (*CE* IV, 235). Such moments of happiness, unfortunately, are usually experienced by Hawthorne's characters in the form of nostalgic memories of a lost plentitude, and Hawthorne explicitly excludes himself from such reciprocal relations by making sympathy a primary force in a world to which he does not belong. In his case a preference for solitude combines with "some witchcraft or other" to break the ordinary tie with humanity. The peculiar circumstances of his youth, he believes, have conditioned him in such a way that he can exist without the "oxygen of sympathy" required to sustain the lives of other men: "But I am of somewhat sterner stuff and tougher fibre . . . and the dark seclusion—the atmosphere without any oxygen of sympathy—in which I spent all the years of my youthful manhood, has enabled me to do almost as well without as with it" (*EN*, 256). Hawthorne apparently does not require the reciprocity that sustains the lives of other men. As a result of his own peculiar circumstances, the waves of sympathy that flow from him are not the expression of purely personal feelings, not a manifestation of self generated by the sympathy of others and requiring a sympathetic response, but are a sympathetic description of human nature in general. His "involuntary reserve," as he calls it, allows him to sympathize with others in a general way but prevents a revelation of self capable of eliciting a corresponding response from others. The "objectivity" of his writing, therefore, is the natural result of his relation to the world, a relationship which is primarily a visual one. He sees the world but is not engaged by it. It is present to him, but he is not drawn into its presence, with the result that the reality of others is disclosed without the direct disclosure of the writer's own reality.

The narrative perspective in Hawthorne's fiction expresses in an obvious way this curious relationship to others. Consider, for example, the unusual perspective of the narrator of "The Old Apple-Dealer": "Thus unconsciously to myself, and unsuspected by him, I have studied the old apple-dealer, until he has become a naturalized citizen of my inner world. How little would he imagine—poor, neglected, friendless, unappreciated, and with little that demands appreciation—that the mental eye of an utter stranger has so often reverted to his figure" (*CE* X, 439). *Unconsciously to myself and unsuspected by him:* in this unusual way originates the act of perception in Hawthorne's world. Naked selfhood is here provided with a double veil that protects it, first, from one's own gaze, for the contents of the mind are not put into question by any epistemological inquiry (the process which makes the old man a part of the narrator's internal world is an unconscious one); and second, from the gaze of the other, for the apple dealer is not aware that he is being watched. The threads of the "cloudy veil" that form the frontier separating the self from the rest of the world are intricately interwoven with those that form the barrier protecting the self from the "dark labyrinth of mind" (*CE* I, 166). Hawthorne's detachment, in other words, is at once imposed on him and willed by him. The result is that he wishes to live neither within the realm of interior space nor in that occupied by other people. He idealizes neither the solitude of the romantic recluse who withdraws from the world to carry on an exclusive commerce with himself nor the shared intimacy of life with other people: "The most desirable mode of existence might be that of a spiritualized Paul Pry, hovering invisible round man and woman, witnessing their deeds, searching into their hearts, borrowing brightness from their felicity, and shade from their sorrow, and retaining no emotion peculiar to himself" (*CE* IX, 192).

This passage expresses nicely the desire born of Hawthorne's curious relationship with the world, because it idealizes a state of existence where the self is not subject to the law of reciprocity. Because Paul Pry is invisible and

without any emotion peculiar to himself, he is free to experience others without becoming in turn an object of their
experience. Like Browning, Hawthorne seems to extend the
romantic idea of the sympathetic imagination from material
objects to other people, a strategy that in both writers is
linked to an excessive desire for privacy.[2] With Hawthorne
as with Browning there is evidence of a remarkable ability
for "throwing [himself] mentally into situations foreign to
[his] own, and detecting, with a cheerful eye, the desirable
circumstances of each" (*CE* IX, 352). Both his daughter
and son remark on his ability to make "himself all things to
men" (*CW* XI, 469),[3] and he endows many of the artist
figures in his fiction with this important quality. Coverdale,
for example, speaks of his impulse "to live in other lives, or
to endeavor—by generous sympathies, by delicate intuitions
[to bring] my human spirit into manifold accordance with
the companions whom God assigned me" (*CE* III, 160).

As Hawthorne recognizes, however, the ideal circumstances described in the Paul Pry passage are impossible.
Man is not invisible; nor is he able completely to empty

---

[2] J. Hillis Miller describes Browning's distinctive contribution to
romanticism as his extension of the idea of sympathetic imagination
from natural objects to other people (*The Disappearance of God*
[Cambridge: Harvard University Press, 1963], p. 106).

[3] Julian Hawthorne wrote of his father: "Now Hawthorne, both
by nature and by training was of a disposition to throw himself
imaginatively into the shoes (as the phrase is) of whatever person
happened to be his companion. For the time being, he would seem
to take their point of view and to speak their language" *Hawthorne
and His Wife* [Cambridge: James R. Osgood, 1884], I, p. 88. See
also the discussion of this same ability in Rose Hawthorne Lathrop's
Memories of Hawthorne (Boston: Houghton, Mifflin, 1897), pp.
198–200.

himself, to become a pure consciousness of others. He has a body that is at once his point of view upon the world and, at the same time, the object that makes him visible to other people. Consequently, if he is to approach the spiritualized Paul Pry ideal he must first find a way to watch others without being seen himself. Hawthorne's attempt to accomplish such a goal is expressed by the recurrent motif of spying in his fiction. His own circumstances and the nature of existence cause him to see the world (as he wrote to Longfellow) as through a "peep-hole,"[4] and he frequently presents a scene in which one character watches another without being seen, or watches from a high window, a tree, or hill, or studies a reflection in a mirror. Each seeks to be a "watchman, all-heeding and unheeded" (*CE* IX, 192), to be "unseen of men . . . even while standing in their eyes" (*CE* III, 184).

Some of Hawthorne's narrators manage to attain the invisibility and nonreciprocal sympathy posited as the ideal form of existence by the narrator of "Sights from a Steeple." The story of *The House of the Seven Gables*, for example, is told by a "disembodied listener" (*CE* II, 30) who can see and hear everyone but who cannot, in turn, be seen or heard by them. Interestingly, however, the first-person narrators do not possess this same freedom. Like the speaker in "Sights from a Steeple" they must "descend" at last from their lofty post and "resume [their] station on lower earth" (*CE* IX, 198). They are, as Henry James noted of Coverdale, "particular" men "with a certain hu-

---

[4] Letter dated Salem, June 4th, 1837, in *The Portable Hawthorne*, Malcolm Cowley (New York: Viking Press, 1969), p. 669.

man grossness."[5] They can be seen by others, and, more importantly, they possess emotions similar to those of the people they describe. The narrator of "Night Sketches," a "looker on in life," weaves a "pathetic story" of the "fate" of drowned lovers but in the process must face the fact that "my fate is hard that I should be wandering homeless here, taking to my bosom night and storm and solitude, instead of wife and children" (*CE* IX, 430–431).

As James apparently recognized, these first-person narrators—Coverdale in particular—point to Hawthorne's realization that the "structure of the world demands that we cannot see without being visible"[6] and yet, at the same time, express his desire to "shrink into the nearest obscurity" rather than "any longer seeking to live in the sight of the world" (*CE* III, 184). Although he is visible to others and more emotionally involved in the events he witnesses than he chooses to admit, Coverdale nevertheless seeks to derive his emotional and mental sustenance from the activities he views from a distance. He is anxious to sympathize with others "as a chorus in a classic play" (97) without becoming himself an object of sympathy. Hence he tries to aestheticize his surroundings at Blithedale—to "turn the affair into a ballad" (*CE* III, 33)—by viewing them from a detached position. Perhaps then they will be "etherealized by distance" (*CE* V, 138), transformed by his perspective into "dreamwork and enchantment" (*CE* III, 213).

This attempt to use the distancing power of the imagination to modify the situation where reference to the other is

[5] Henry James, *Hawthorne* (Garden City: Doubleday, n.d.), pp. 112–113.
[6] Sartre, p. 293.

also reference to the self is characteristic of Hawthorne. His hope is that his art will allow him to realize his desire to participate in the lives of others and at the same time protect him from becoming the object of others' attention. After all, it enables him to hold others at a distance and to represent in words the patterns of the lives of those who have fascinated him.

Such an approach, however, suggests that detachment may not be the result of an involuntary, instinctive act that expresses a condition natural to the mind. Rather, it implies that such a perspective may be a form of enchantment generated by the desire to enjoy a privileged relation with the world. In other words, distance for Hawthorne is not the source of desire. Desire for him is dialectical in the sense that its objects are always testimonies in reverse to the value of the condition which initiated it. It is the energy that both generates enchantments and destroys them, transforms the cold hillside into enchanted ground and then reverses the procedure.

As a mere object of sight, nothing is more deficient in picturesque features than a procession, seen in its passage through narrow streets. The spectator feels it to be a fool's play, when he can distinguish the tedious common-place of each man's visage, with the perspiration and weary self-importance on it, and the very cut of his pantaloons, and the stiffness or laxity of his shirt-collar, and the dust on the back of his black coat. In order to become majestic, it should be viewed from some vantage-point, as it rolls its slow and long array through the centre of a wide plain, or the stateliest public square of a city; for then, by its remoteness, it melts all the petty personalities, of which it is made up, into one broad mass of existence—one great life—one collected body of mankind, with a vast, homogeneous spirit animating it. But, on the other hand, if an impressible person, standing alone over the brink of one of these processions, should behold it, not in its atoms, but in its aggregate—as a mighty river of life, massive in its tide, and black with mystery, and, out of its depth, calling to the kindred depth within him—then the contiguity would add to the effect. It might so fascinate him, that he would hardly be restrained from plunging into the surging stream of human sympathies. [*CE* II, 165]

If seen from a detached point of view, life no longer seems petty and oppressive. Distance purifies and idealizes it by rescuing it from the harsh fierceness of the actual, from the ugly and oppressive facticity which costumes and conventions merely accentuate. Moreover, as it purifies the objects of sight, distance also relieves the spectator of the burdens of the actual world. To live in the world is to grow "hard and rough," to be covered with "earthly dust," and to have one's "heart made callous by rude encounters with the multitude" (*LL* I, 224). Such is Hawthorne's experience when he leaves the solitude of the Old Manse for the public world of the Custom House. Here the materiality of life presses so intrusively on the spectator that he is overcome by the same weariness that burdens those who form the procession of life. He is forced to live as they do, to adopt their perspective. Consequently he faces becoming himself an actor in the fool's play, a role that carries with it obvious dangers. For to participate in the empty masquerade is to run the risk of having one's consciousness "attenuated of much of its proper substance, and diffused among many alien interests" (*CE* III, 157). The first symptom of this transformation is a thickening and clouding of the imaginative faculty. The mirror of the imagination becomes tarnished by the oppressive atmosphere of the world. The mind becomes thick and heavy, for the intellect seems to be "dwindling away; or exhaling, without your consciousness, like ether out of a phial; so that, at every glance, you find a smaller and less volatile residuum" (*CE* I, 38).

This horrible transformation can be resisted only by imposing a distance between oneself and the world, by seeking a "safe and inaccessible seclusion" (*CE* V, 187). Living in "snug seclusion" (*CE* X, 5), one is protected from the materiality that surrounds and threatens those who live in the midst of others. In solitude one gains the "freedom to think, and dream and feel" (*LL* I, 213–214). The "heavy breath" of Rome laden with malaria "[can] not aspire" (*CE* IV, 327) to the heights of Hilda's tower; Coverdale's tree hermitage "symbolize[s] [his] individuality and aid[s] [him] in keeping it inviolate" (*CE* III, 99); the seclusion of his second-story room makes it possible for the narrator of "Sunday at Home" to send his "inner man" to church "while many, whose bodily presence fills the accustomed seats, have left their souls at home" (*CE* IX, 21); and, finally, Hester Prynne, living in her isolated cottage at the edge of the forest, is able to become for the first time the ground of her own being; "the world's law was no law for her mind" (*CE* I, 164).

The freedom experienced by Hawthorne and his characters as they stand within the "magic boundaries" of solitude, "kept from the contact of actual life, so that its sounds and tumult [seem] remote" (*DGS*, 284), however, does not rest on a secure ground. Because it derives from the "absorbing spell" (*CE* IX, 149) of distance, it is a form of hallucination subject to the disenchanting pull of desire.

As the "parade of life" passage suggests, the enchantment of distance may result in an unusual reversal of attitude. That which once seemed petty and oppressive may become majestic and magnetic; that which has been the most dreaded may suddenly become the most longed for; "persons who have wandered, or been expelled, out of the common track of things, even were it for a better system, desire nothing so much as to be led back. They shiver in their loneliness, be it on a mountain-top or in a dungeon" (*CE* II, 140). For Hawthorne, man cannot safely remain long removed from the world of other men. He feels truly alive only when he is experienced as such by others. "This perception of an infinite, shivering solitude, amid which we cannot come close enough to human beings to be warmed by them, and where they turn to cold, chilly shapes of mist, is one of the most forlorn results of any accident, misfortune, crime, or peculiarity of character that puts an individual ajar with the world" (*CE* IV, 113).

The act of distancing, then, suddenly is seen as a disruption between man and total reality, a disruption which deprives him of the life-giving warmth of other people. That perspective which originally had seemed to purify the world and to free man from the burden of facticity has instead estranged him from his fellow man and made him a foreigner in his own land. For if involvement in the "common business of life" threatens to solidify consciousness, withdrawal from it robs man of his substance and transforms him into "chilly shapes of mist." The realm of solitude "makes the spirit shiver as if it had reached the frozen solitudes around the pole" (*CE* X, 459). Hence to remove oneself from the parade of life is to be converted "from an interested actor into a cold and disconnected spectator of all of mankind's warm and sympathetic life" (*CW* XI, 296–297).

But a return to the world would only momentarily revitalize. As Hawthorne's Custom House experience indicates, involvement with others generates a desire for solitude with the same insistency that solitude creates a longing for others. On the one hand a dread of becoming wholly substance; on the other a fear of being nothing but shadow; linking both the power of the other. Here is the creative source of Hawthorne's imagination: an unappeasable desire, the experience of fulfillment of which is necessarily illusory and temporary and which therefore produces an alternating movement from enchantment to disenchantment and back again. This is the basic structure of Hawthorne's world, a structure which, as we shall see, helps to explain why he became a writer and what relation to the world his writings express.

2

The Enchantment of the Other

Moreover, we cannot give an undistorted account of "a person" without giving an account of his relation with others. Even an account of one person cannot afford to forget that each person is always *acting upon* others and *acted upon* by others. The others are there also. No one acts or experiences in a vacuum. The person whom we describe, and over whom we theorize, *is not the only agent in his "world."* How he perceives and acts towards the others, how they perceive and act towards him, how he perceives them as perceiving him, how they perceive him as perceiving them, are all aspects of "the situation." They are all pertinent to understanding one person's participation in it.

A woman cannot be a mother without a child. She needs a child to give her the identity of a mother. . . . All "identities" require an other: some other in and through a relationship with whom self-identity is actualized.

R. D. Laing, Self and Others

Man's relationship to other people takes several forms in Hawthorne's world, and he expresses these relationships through the use of a set of motifs which recur so often in his writing that they furnish its underlying structure. The related motifs of the sphere, the gaze, and the veil, among others, express in Hawthorne's world the possible ways human beings are related to one another. These thematic strands, however, exist within the general web of what one might call (to borrow a word from Ortega) man's circumstances. For Hawthorne, man's relations to other people are modified to some extent by the context in which they occur, a context which consists of the natural, the historical, and the social. Human relationships, in other words, always take place in a world with a horizon that is the sign of a complicated structure.

For Hawthorne, as for most of his American contemporaries, nature and culture are not experienced so much as polarities based on the autonomy of the human world as they are viewed as warring opposites one of which must inevitably destroy the other. For Hawthorne, however, the conflict is neither as dangerous as it is for Melville, nor as potentially tragic as it is for Cooper. Hawthornian man is successful in his attempt to humanize the world, and he seldom questions the impulses that move him in that direction. He enters the "dreary and perilous wilderness" (*CE* II, 150), imposes on it his own will and design, and transforms it, little by little, until finally it gives way to a world made in his image and subject to his control. For Hawthorne, as for Cooper, the "pathless forest . . . give[s] place—as it inevitably must . . . to the golden fertility of human culture" (18). Unlike Cooper, however, Hawthorne finds no sign of Divine presence in the "great black forest" (*CE* I, 203). On the contrary, this dreary and perilous wilderness is an image of the godless world into which the "original Adam had been expelled" (*CE* II, 150). Here one encounters a "wild heathen Nature . . . never subjugated by human law, nor illumined by higher truth" (*CE* I, 203). The central drama in his world, therefore, does not derive from the act whereby man transforms the wilderness but from the problematical and perilous relationship between the human world and its wild source. To leave the "narrowness of human limits" and to enter the "vast, undefined space" (*CE* III, 36) must be to renounce in one way or another the values of culture. Young Goodman Brown enters the "heart of the dark wilderness" and, like Conrad's Marlow, never again is able to see the human world in the same way: "A stern, a sad, a darkly meditative, a distrustful, if not a desperate man did he become from the night of that fearful dream" (*CE* X, 89). In a similar way culture suddenly loses its authenticity for Hester Prynne when her sin "converted forest-land, still so uncongenial to every other pilgrim and wanderer, into [her] wild and dreary, but life-long home" (*CE* I, 80). "Her intellect and heart had their home, as it were, in desert places, where she roamed as freely as the wild Indian in his woods. For years past she had looked from this estranged point of view at human institutions, and whatever priests or legislators had established; criticizing all with hardly more reverence than the Indian would feel for the clerical band, the judicial robe, the pillory, the gallows, the fireside, or the church" (199).

Both Goodman Brown and Hester discover that civilization—moral and social laws as well as physical comforts, all of man's shelters and disciplines—is a structure which when seen from the outside has no essential solidity. From this point of view culture is the result of a kind of an enchantment, a process whereby the "black art" (127) of the forest is tamed and domesticated by a simpler but more powerful form of magic: "homely witchcraft." "A wild hut of underbrush, tossed together by wayfarers through the primitive forest, would acquire the home-aspect by one night's lodging of such a woman [Phoebe], and would retain it, long after her quiet figure had disappeared into the surrounding shade" (*CE* II, 172). Phoebe's "natural magic" is a metaphor for man's ability to force the world to take his shape. Magical too is the wizard, Matthew Maule, who "with his own toil . . . had hewn out of the primeval forest" an acre or two "to be his garden-ground and homestead" (7), only to be executed for witchcraft, and his descendent, Holgrave, who "moulds gloomy shapes" out of "shapeless gloom" (306), is also something of a magician.

In a certain sense, then, Hawthorne's culture is what Ortega calls a frontier culture, a wild one without a sense of permanence and security.[1] Because it is the result of an enchantment, the culture is both uncertain and problematical. Like seventeenth-century Boston it exists "on the edge of the Western wilderness" (*CE* I, 57), near the darkness it

[1] José Ortega y Gasset, *Meditations on Quixote*, trans. Evelyn Rugg and Diego Marin (New York: Norton, 1961), pp. 94–95.

seeks to enlighten but which at any moment may invade its borders. Dimmesdale, returning from his memorable meeting with Hester in the forest, is confronted by an unexplainable transformation in the world from which he has been absent for only a day.

As he drew near the town, he took an impression of change from the series of familiar objects that presented themselves. It seemed not yesterday, not one, nor two, but many days, or even years ago, since he had quitted them. There, indeed, was each former trace of the street, as he remembered it, and all the peculiarities of the houses, with the due multitude of gable-peaks, and a weathercock at every point where his memory suggested one. Not the less, however, came this importunately obstrusive sense of change. . . . A similar impression struck him most remarkably, as he passed under the walls of his own church. The edifice had so very strange, and yet so familiar, an aspect, that Mr. Dimmesdale's mind vibrated between two ideas; either that he had seen it only in a dream hitherto, or that he was merely dreaming about it now.
   This phenomenon, in the various shapes which it assumed, indicated no external change, but so sudden and important a change in the spectator of the familiar scene, that the intervening space of a single day had operated on his consciousness like the lapse of years. The minister's own will, and Hester's will, and the fate that grew between them, had wrought this transformation.   [*CE* I, 216–217]

The minister, like Hester, has breathed the "wild, free atmosphere of an unredeemed unchristianizd, lawless region" and now has a "knowledge of hidden mysteries" (201), a suspicion that society may rest on no transcendent ground but may be merely the magical creation of man's will.

   Hawthorne's vision, however, is not as close to Melville's as the above texts seem to suggest. While there are elements of his thought that resemble those of Melville and the post-romantics Melville anticipates, there are equally important aspects associating Hawthorne with some of his less adventurous contemporaries. If the desert places of the New World make the human realm seem mutable and dreamlike, some sense of solidity and stability may be regained by turning away from the "boundless forest" toward the "broad pathway of the sea" (*CE* I, 197) and reminding ourselves of Our Old Home. Our true origins, after all, are not in the "rude and untamed landscape of the Western World" (*CE* IV, 71) but in the carefully cultivated and domesticated nature of the Old World. Here the natural world is not a place alien to man and does not point to the ephemeral quality of things human. Just the reverse is true. In the English forests one gets the impression that man has made a permanent place for himself in the world: "The spot was an entanglement of boughs, and yet did not give him the impression of wildness; for it was the stranger's idea that everything, in this long cultivated region, had been touched and influenced by man's care, every oak, every bush, every sod, that man knew them all, and that they knew him, and by that mutual knowledge had become other than they were in the first freedom of growth, such as may be found in an American forest" (*DGS*, 275).

There was a time, of course, "when England's forests were as wild as those of America," but that was so long ago that it is almost forgotten. The forest now seems a "conquered and regulated wilderness," a place where even the deer retain a "free forest citizenship" and yet are in "some sense subject to man" (95). Crucial here is the sense that "present being is incorporated with the past" (*CE* IX, 293–

294), that the past is serving as a "foundation for the present, to keep it from vibrating and being blown away with every breeze" (*DGS*, 82). Man has been able to transfigure the forest in a permanent and essential way as a result of having cared for it for such a long time. In these surroundings the individual does not have the impression that he is a first man; others have been here before him, and the sense of their presence gives him a feeling of belonging to an established and progressive enterprise.

This Old World view of the relation between man and nature is an especially interesting one to Hawthorne, and he explores its implications in a number of different ways. It is present, for example, in the various gardens in his writings, those "nooks and crannies where Nature, like a stray partridge, hides her head among the long established haunts of men" (*CE* III, 149). Gardens are human creations, but they usually express man's willingness to leave nature "to her own ways and methods" by bestowing only enough care "to prevent wildness from growing into deformity" (*CE* IV, 72).[2] Most of Hawthorne's gardens suggest that man and nature can coexist. The trees, plants, and vines growing between Coverdale's hotel and the fashionable apartments in which he is so interested are in a "situation . . . warm and sheltered . . . where the soil has doubtless been enriched to a more than natural fertility" (*CE* III, 148). Here a cat retains "all the privileges of forest-life, in the close heart of city conventionalisms" as she pursues the birds who live in the trees, while they, in turn, know how

[2] The obvious exception here, of course, is Rappaccini's garden, an example of what can happen when man tries to twist nature to fit his unnatural desires.

to protect themselves from her wiles because they are of "city breeding" (149). And, as man's creations here shelter and protect nature, in the Pyncheon garden nature provides a "breathing place" (*CE* II, 87) for the rural Phoebe, the wanderer Holgrave, and the aesthete Clifford.

Reciprocity between man and nature then seems possible in Hawthorne's world. As a matter of fact, at times he seems to assert that there are elements found in both man and nature which imply a common ground. In the preface to *Mosses from an Old Manse*, for example, he implies an analogous relationship between the two when he writes, on the one hand, that "childless men, if they would know something of the bliss of paternity, should plant a seed" (*CE* X, 13), and, on the other, refers to nature as "our Mother" (27). Such assertions of similitude, however, derive their thrust from the power of enchantment that transforms the realm of the Old Manse into a "fairyland" (33), "the Enchanted Ground" (28) of which casts over Hawthorne the "spell of a tranquil spirit" (29). If man and nature happily coexist in Hawthorne's gardens, they do so not because they share traits which bring them close to and cause them to resemble one another; rather the relationship is the result of man's discovery that nature loses its value if it is totally humanized. Gardens are the result of a happy balance between identity and difference: "An orchard has a relation to mankind, and readily connects itself with matters of the heart. The trees possess a domestic character; they have lost the wild nature of their forest-kindred, and have grown humanized by receiving the care of man, as well as by contributing to his wants" (*CE* X, 12). The orchard and man are related not because the same pattern lies hidden beneath the surface of each, pulling them magnetically to one another. On the contrary, the relationship is grounded on man's initial recognition of a basic difference between the two and his subsequent attempt to minimize the difference by partially humanizing the natural. Such humanization, grounded on difference rather than resemblance, is more concretely expressed in those objects in Hawthorne's world which through human use have become almost alive themselves. The "aspect" of the House of the Seven Gables is "like a human countenance" (*CE* II, 5) and is itself like a "great human heart, with a life of its own, and full of rich and sombre reminiscences" (27). Like the Old Manse, the house seems to have been transformed simply because "so much of mankind's varied experience had passed there" (27). In a similar way, the Scarlet Letter, having been worn so many years on Hester's breast, has become the repository of "some deep meaning . . . most worthy of interpretation" (*CE* I, 31).

Hawthorne feels most at home in a world where the process of humanization has long since taken place and now endures in the objects created by other men in the distant past. Much of the Edenic atmosphere of the honeymoon years at the Old Manse is generated by the house and grounds which have been permeated by the lives of past inhabitants: "We dwell in an old moss-covered mansion, and tread in the worn footprints of the past, and have a gray clergyman's ghost for our daily and nightly inmate" (*CE* X, 153). Outside is a grave "marked by a small, mossgrown fragment of stone at the head and another at the foot" (9), which releases a vision of the battle that marked the beginning of the Revolution, and partially buried in the soil are stone relics which call up scenes of some "unknown age, before the white man came" (19).

There is an exquisite delight, too, in picking up, for one's self, an arrow-head that was dropt centuries ago, and has never been handled since, and which we thus receive directly from the hand of the red hunter, who purposed to shoot it at his game or at an enemy. Such an incident builds up again the Indian village, amid its encircling forest, and recalls to life the painted chiefs and warriors, the squaws at their household toil, and the children sporting among the wigwams, while the little wind-rocked pappoose swings from the branch of the tree. [11]

Both the house and grounds are the repositories of history, for they are filled with objects made by men of other generations which still retain something of the human touch that created them. In a similar way the House of the Seven Gables retains the "fragrance" of Alice Pyncheon's "delightful character . . . as a dried rosebud scents the drawer where it has withered and perished" (*CE* II, 83).

In such a world a man with an active imagination might well remain in solitude, at a distance from those living the life of the "passing moment" (*CE* II, 24), and still be a part of a complex human world. Old Esther Dudley and the Province House Story Teller are removed from the ordinary world, but they are certainly not alone. The past, preserved as it is in the parts of nature man has reshaped, may release him from the necessity of performing an active role in the present moment. This possibility is explored in a number of Hawthorne's works but nowhere more persistently than in *The Marble Faun*. As the preface makes clear, the novel itself is the product of "Ruin" (*CE* IV, 3), that is to say antiquity. And, indeed, Rome, the Eternal City, like

Egdon Heath in *The Return of the Native*, is the primary force in the book. Only here does one have that "vague sense of ponderous remembrances; a perception of such weight and density in a by-gone life, of which this spot was the centre, that the present moment is pressed down or crowded out, and our individual affairs and interests are but half as real, here, as elsewhere. . . . Side by side with the massiveness of the Roman Past, all matters, that we handle or dream of, now-a-days, look evanescent and visionary alike" (6).

Here, apparently, man is freed from the ugliness and weariness that direct involvement in the business of life usually brings and yet does not suffer the subsequent chill experienced by so many of Hawthorne's characters when they find themselves similarly removed from the stream of things. Life in Rome is a "day-dream" (70) and, as a result, the city is a "favorite residence of artists—their ideal home, which they sigh for, in advance, and are so loth to migrate from, after once breathing its enchanted air" (132). Here is "shadow," "antiquity," and "mystery," which together form a "sort of poetic or fairy precinct, where actualities [are not] so terribly insisted upon, as they are, and must needs be, in America" (3). Like the "beckoning shadows at the ancient windows of the ancestral home" (*DGS*, 261) those of Rome create a "land of enchantment" (147), a place where men can live "in a half waking dream, partly conscious of the fantastic nature of their ideas, yet with these ideas almost as real to them as the facts of the natural world" (221).

As Hawthorne's language suggests, however, man's sense of being at home in the Old World is the result of an en-

chantment cast over him by history, and, like all such enchantments, it carries the seeds of its own destruction. The
shadows of the past like those of the mind are easily converted into substance. For Holgrave the past is not a sign
that man has managed successfully to humanize the world;
it is an assertion of his tie to the material world, and as such
is "odious and abominable" (*CE* II, 184). "It lies upon the
present like a giant's dead body" (182). Similarly, the Eternal City is disenchanted by the "sheer weight and density"
(*CE* IV, 6) of a "long decaying corpse" (325). Here it
seems as if all the "weary and dreary past were piled upon
the back of the Present" (302). This aspect of the past is
dramatized in *The Marble Faun* by Miriam's model, the
ghostlike spectre who first appears in that "vast tomb" (24),
the Catacomb of Saint Calixtus, and whose "shadow" is
"always flung into the light which Miriam diffused around
her" (36). But he is even more frightening in death than in
life. When Miriam is confronted by his dead face in the
Church of the Capuchins, the "misty substance" which
seems to surround her is transformed into "solid, stony substance" (82). In seeking to create a "new sphere" (431) for
herself in the enchanted atmosphere of Rome, Miriam hopes
to escape forever the shadow of her own past. Instead she
"went astray in it, and wandered . . . into crime" (430).
The "spell of ruin" (409) can offer no real release from the
weight of everyday life, for the past does not really offer
an escape from the present moment; rather it burdens it
with its own "ponderous gloom" (410). "And what locali-
ties for new crime existed in those guilty sites, where the
crime of departed ages used to be at home, and had its long,
hereditary haunt. . . . It prolonged the tendency to crime,

and developed an instantaneous growth of it, wherever an opportunity was found" (412).

The relics of the past from this point of view are not simply generators of a harmless enchantment but possess a coercive power capable of shaping people's lives. Such an accumulation of history makes it impossible for "each generation [to have] only its own sins and sorrows to bear" (302). Several generations of Pyncheons suffer under the burden of the Maules' curse and the evil ghost of Colonel Pyncheon, and Hawthorne is bound to Salem because his ancestors were born and died there and "have mingled their earthly substance with the soil; until no small portion of it must necessarily be akin to the mortal frame wherewith, for a little while, I walk the streets" (*CE* I, 9).

In this perception the natural, historical, and social realms combine to produce a context to which man is bound but in which he can never feel at home. "Home feeling" (*CW* X, 484) may be experienced, but it is never any more than a momentary illusion, the result of some form of enchantment. Much the same may be said for man's relation to society when it is considered, as it must be, in terms of its relations to nature and to history. At times Hawthorne is bewitched by his "passion for thronged streets and the intense bustle of human life" (*EN*, 591). For example, he is drawn to the poorer streets of Liverpool by the "bustle, a sense of being in the midst of life, and of having got hold of something real" (*EN*, 13). But such a response is a mystification created by a desire which springs from a perception of his own solitude. With familiarity comes an awareness of the "thick, foggy, stifled elements of cities, the entangled life of many men together" (*CE* III, 146).

It [London] is human life; it is this material world; it is a grim and heavy reality. I have never had the same sense of being surrounded by materialisms, and hemmed in with the grossness of this earthly life, anywhere else; . . . it is really an ungladdened life, to wander through these huge, thronged ways, over a pavement foul with mud, ground into it by a million of footsteps; jostling against people who do not seem to be individuals, but all one mass . . . the roar of vehicles pervading me, wearisome cabs and omnibusses [*sic*]; everywhere, the dingy brick edifices heaving themselves up, and shutting out all but a strip of sullen cloud that serves London for a sky;—in short, a general impression of grime and sordidness, and, at this season, always a fog scattered along the vista of streets, sometimes so densely as almost to spiritualize the materialism and make the scene resemble the other world of worldly people, gross even in ghostliness. [*EN*, 607]

The city, which from one point of view could be seen as the most convincing expression of man's control over nature, of his spiritual and imaginative prowess, expresses instead the extent to which he is bound to and imprisoned in matter. Like the enchantment of history, that of the city is demystified by an overwhelming sense of man's tie to the material world, and that sense is generated to a large extent by the threatening presence of others. He feels as caught and coerced by the collective and the public as the residents of Rome are by the relics of the past. Life in the city is a clear indication that man's incarnation involves more than the imprisonment of the mind in flesh; it entails, too, the imprisonment of the mind in the usages and institutions of the social matrix.

Laws, institutions, religions, and the arts, all of these forms are tested and found wanting in the four major novels. "Daily custom" is shown to be a "stone-wall" which "grows about us" and "consolidates itself into almost as material an entity as mankind's strongest architecture" (*CE* X, 362). From the Puritan society of *The Scarlet Letter* where men live "petrified" into a "grim rigidity" (*CE* I, 49), to that of *The House of the Seven Gables* which is grounded on the "big, heavy, solid unrealities, such as gold, landed estate, offices of trust, and emolument, and public houses" (*CE* II, 229), to the "worldly society" of *The Blithedale Romance* where a "cold skepticism smothers what it can of our spiritual aspirations and makes the rest ridiculous" (*CE* III, 101), to the "little life of Rome pressed down by the weight of death" (*CW* X, 484–485), Hawthorne emphasizes the "thousand follies, fripperies, prejudices, habits, and other such worldly dust as inevitably settles upon the crowd along the broad highway, giving them all one sordid aspect" (*CE* III, 61).

It is this perception of the "weary tread-mill of the established system" (*CE* III, 19) which generates the theme of social change running throughout Hawthorne's writing. Hester Prynne's belief in a time when "a new truth would be revealed, in order to establish the whole relation between man and woman on a surer ground of mutual happiness" (*CE* I, 263), and the commitment which motivates the members of the Blithedale Community are two examples of the impulse toward social change governing a number of Hawthorne's characters. But the implications of the theme are explored in fullest detail in Hawthorne's account of the history of the House of the Seven Gables.

"The House of the Seven Gables, antique as it now looks, was not the first habitation erected by civilized man, on precisely the same spot of ground" (*CE* II, 6). Prior to the "stately mansion" (13) which was built to "assume its rank among the habitations of mankind" (11), was the presocial hut of the solitary pioneer. Built by the "original occupant of the soil" (6) in a space "hewn out of the primeval forest, to be his garden-ground and homestead," this "rude hovel" (7) was the essential habitation. "Remote from what was then the centre of the village" (6–7), it was not conceived as a place which opened to the world of other men. Rather it was an expression of the pioneering spirit, of man's belief in his ability to master the fact of his aloneness in an alien world. The solitary hut was an image of man's confrontation with nature, designed as it was to protect him from the heat of the sun and the fury of the storms. It was a place of refuge and solitude, a small human outpost in the midst of the "dark, inscrutable forest" (*CE* I, 79).

The thatched hut was destroyed, although not by the natural forces which menaced it. It resisted the storms of nature, but it could not withstand the "iron energy of purpose" of a "prominent and powerful personage, who asserted plausible claims to the proprietorship of this, and a large adjacent tract of land, on the strength of a grant from the legislature" (*CE* II, 7). Society itself is what truly threatens the pioneering spirit, for it destroys individualism by turning it into the demonic. Matthew Maule was accused of and executed for witchcraft and that circumstance became the justification for society's appropriating and reconsecrating the space he had carved from the wilderness; "it was a death that blasted with strange horror the humble name of the dweller in the cottage, and made it seem almost a religious act to drive the plough over the little area of his habitation, and obliterate his place and memory from among men" (7).

This was the act of men who live, as Charles Feidelson has said, in a world removed from God and definable only in terms of that distance.[3] For although God was gone he had left behind a hierarchical, feudalistic social system which was an adequate reminder of his power and justice. In the Puritan community "religion and law were almost identical" (*CE* I, 50); "the forms of its authority were felt to possess the sacredness of divine institutions" (64). The social structure, in other words, was dignified by divine sanction. Hence "the great man of the town was commonly called King, and his wife—not Queen, to be sure—but Lady" (*CE* II, 63).

Because the forms of society were supported by a power outside themselves there existed an elaborate set of hereditary legitimacies and distinctions: "These names of gentleman and lady had a meaning . . . and conferred privileges, desirable, or otherwise, on those entitled to bear them" (45). Within this system, then, each man was born to an assigned place to which he must tie himself and submit, for a certain place in the social hierarchy was a God-given right. Hence those people who were born near the top of the social structure were thought of as possessing great expectations. For this reason the Pyncheon family believed in the authenticity of the lost title to a "vast, and as yet unexplored and unmeasured tract of eastern lands" (18).

---

[3] Charles Feidelson, "*The Scarlet Letter*, in *Hawthorne Centenary Essays*, ed. Roy Harvey Pearce (Columbus: Ohio State University Press, 1964), p. 52.

"This impalpable claim, therefore, resulted in nothing more solid than to cherish, from generation to generation, an absurd delusion of family importance, which all along characterized the Pyncheons. It caused the poorest member of the race to feel as if he inherited a kind of nobility, and might yet come into possession of princely wealth to support it" (19).

Even after the Revolution the Pyncheons continued to believe that their lack of status was a horrible accident, that there was a hidden place for them and a dignified and secure role. The mysterious document would be found and the divine right of the family authenticated. This attitude, like the social system that generated it, was not in harmony with the pioneering spirit, for that was founded in the premise that man carved out his own place and any status he attained in the world would be the result of his own efforts. His property was that which he was able to wrestle "from the wild hand of Nature by [his] own sturdy toil." And the "idea of any man's asserting a right—on the strength of mouldy parchments, signed with the faded autographs of governors and legislators, long dead and forgotten" (19) to those lands seemed absurd.

In those pre-revolutionary days, however, the pioneer was doomed; Maule's "humble homestead" (8) was replaced by a "family mansion" (9), designed to "assume its rank among the habitations of mankind" (11). On the day of the "ceremony of consecration, festive, as well as religious" (11), however, the old system began to fade. Although the "solemn festival," where the guests were arranged "with a scrutinizing regard to the high or low degree of each" (12), seemed at first like an expression of the strength of the feudalistic society, the ensuing events were of a nature to invalidate the whole structure of a social order grounded on an extra-human foundation.

Like the other buildings and institutions in the Puritan community the newly constructed house was designed to mediate between a fallen world and a distant God. On the day of the dedication of this "stately mansion" (13), "Pyncheon street . . . was thronged, at the appointed hour, as with a congregation on its way to church" (11). As the people "looked upward" the imposing edifice seemed more a cathedral than a house.

There it rose, a little withdrawn from the line of the street, but in pride, not modesty. Its whole visible exterior was ornamented with quaint figures, conceived in the grotesqueness of a Gothic fancy, and drawn or stamped in the glittering plaster, composed of lime, pebbles, and bits of glass, with which the wood-work of the walls was overspread. On every side, the seven gables pointed sharply towards the sky, and presented the aspect of a whole sisterhood of edifices, breathing through the spiracles of one great chimney. . . .

The principal entrance, which had almost the breadth of a churchdoor, was in the angle between two front gables, and was covered by an open porch, with benches beneath its shelter. [11–12]

But the "founder of this stately mansion" remained "invisible" at his own "solemn festival" (13) and subsequently was discovered "dead, in his new house" (15–16). From this point on, the Pyncheon family, robbed of its progenitor, was supported only by the Colonel's memory, kept alive by the portrait and by the story of the missing deed which would legitimize the family's right to "vast Eastern lands" and restore it to its rightful place in the social hierarchy.

The collapse of the essentialist system, then, was not entirely the result of the curse of the "plebian Maules" (26). The Revolution, to be sure, may at first be seen as the triumph of the spirit of the pioneer over "antique portraits, pedigrees, coats of arms, records and traditions" (38) out of which there emerged a society where the "names of gentleman and lady . . . imply, not privilege, but restriction" (45). The generative source of the Revolution, however, comes from within the system itself. Its seeds were sown when the "forms of authority" became expressions not of divine intent but human will. It was the "personal enmity" (8) lying hidden beneath the Colonel's official acts which doomed him and the system he epitomized. That subterfuge brought into question the belief that society had a supernatural foundation and exposed the possibility that it might, in fact, be a self-generating system.

Revolution, then, is a process of secularization resulting as it does in the destruction of a society based on hereditary legitimacies and distinctions which are dignified by divine sanction. Suddenly God is no longer threateningly distant but completely withdrawn and almost forgotten. The divine perspective is replaced by a human one: "They [Hepzibah and Clifford] pulled open the front-door, and stept across the threshold, and felt, both of them, as if they were standing in the presence of the whole world, and with mankind's great and terrible eye on them alone. The eye of their Father seemed to be withdrawn, and gave them no encouragement" (169). The old society where the sinner most feared the eye of God is no longer; it had been replaced by one where the primary threat comes from the gaze of other people. Nor is it possible to avoid the danger by seeking

direct access to God. Separating heaven from earth is a
wedge of "dull, gray . . . clouds" (266–267) which "symbolize a great, brooding mass of human trouble, doubt, confusion, and chill indifference, between the earth and the
better regions" (245). And the church, center of the old
hierarchical society, has in the new one been allowed to
decay: "At a little distance stood a wooden church, black
with age, and in a dismal state of ruin and decay, with broken
windows, a great rift through the main body of the edifice,
and a rafter dangling from the top of a square tower" (266).

In the place of the old society, where men lived in the
shadow of their dreadful vision of another world, there is
established a city of man dedicated to its own ends: the
problem of getting and spending, the conservation and
acquisition of property. While Colonel Pyncheon believed
in "spiritual ministrations" his descendant, the Judge, believed in "no such nonsense" (278). The Judge fully accepts the view of society implied in his ancestor's using the
forms of authority for personal ends. For him society is not
grounded on some creative force external to itself but is the
product of men who "possess vast ability in grasping, and
arranging, and appropriating to themselves, the big, heavy,
solid unrealities, such as gold, landed estate, offices of trust
and emolument, and public honors" (229). These men—
each with his own good in mind—conspire to establish a vast
system of money-getting dedicated to "the sordid accumulation of copper-coin" (81). The resulting structure is an
autonomous one with its elements referring to nothing outside themselves. As is the case with the "little society"
(163) formed by the figures on the Italian boy's barrel
organ this world is generated by the "excessive desire for

whatever filthy lucre might happen to be in anybody's pocket" (164), "bring[s] nothing finally to pass" (163), and ends in meaningless petrifaction.

Moreover, like the old essentialist order it replaced, this new system, based on the acquisition of money, is a threat to the true individual and to the pioneering spirit. Behind this love of power and money is the "energy of disease" (23); hence both the Colonel and the Judge combine aggressiveness with a predisposition to apoplexy. This aggressive energy is a threat to all who dream of a "house and a moderate garden-spot of one's own" (156), for it seeks to confine the mass of men to the "alms house, as the natural home of their old age" (25). Uncle Venner, for example, "an epitome of times and fashions," speaks of "putting aside business and retiring to my farm . . . the great brick house, you know—the work-house, most folks call it" (62).

The history of the House of the Seven Gables, in effect, is a description of the origins and condition of the society in which man finds himself. It is one that at its beginnings may have been the result of a magical transformation of the wilderness by the will and hand of man, but in its current state it bears as little resemblance to its wild beginnings as the House of the Seven Gables does to Maule's hut. It is characterized, first, by a tendency to accumulate and preserve the ended and the bygone, thereby creating a structure which seems mechanized and dehumanized; and, second, by an aggressive will to power that seeks to materialize or fossilize and to make all interpersonal relationships a conflict of wills. The forms this conflict take are reflected in Hawthorne's world in the motifs of the sphere, the gaze, and the veil.

For Hawthorne every person inhabits a "little sphere of creatures and circumstances, in which he [is] the central object" (*CE* IX, 134), a "narrow circle in which his dreams are recognized" (*CE* I, 27). Each person, in effect, is a perceptual center around which there is a circumference made up of the objects and people which fall within the field of perception. Although grouped and synthesized from a particular point of view, the "creatures and circumstances" are as essential a part of the spherical whole, as is the centralizing force itself. These individual units or groupings, individual "men, in their various spheres" (*CE* I, 249), are linked one to another, thereby forming increasingly larger circumferences around centers composed of experiences or traits shared by various individuals. Hence there is the "sphere of yesterday" (*CE* IV, 410), the "sphere of ordinary womanhood" (*CE* III, 190), the "sphere of human charities" (*CE* I, 81), and, finally, the "sphere of humanity" (*CE* IV, 64). And beyond these known spheres there may be others having a different ontological atmosphere, "another state of existence close beside the little spheres of warmth and light in which we are prattlers and bustlers of a moment" (*CE* III, 37). These invisible spheres are unknowable, and we can only speculate about their existence, as Hawthorne does in a conversation with Hiram Powers: "We reasoned high about other states of being; and I suggested the possibility that there might be beings inhabiting this earth, contemporaneously with us, and close beside us, but of whose existence and whereabout we could have no perception, nor they of ours, because we are endowed with different sets of senses" (*CW* X, 376).

For Hawthorne, then, "individuals are . . . nicely adjusted to a system, and systems to one another and to a whole" (*CE* IX, 140). Such an arrangement, however, is not without problems. To begin with, the fact that an individual enjoys a "connecting link with the rest of human life" (*CW* XI, 32) means that his sphere is open to the influences of the spheres of others, and there is no guarantee that individual spheres are compatible with one another. Clifford Pyncheon, for example, is too "delicate" and "fine" to be "perfectly appreciated by one whose sphere lay so much in the Actual as Phoebe's did" (*CE* II, 140). The same delicacy, moreover, makes him vulnerable to the rougher spheres of others: "He had no right to be a martyr; and, beholding him so fit to be happy, and so feeble for all other purposes, a generous, strong, and noble spirit, would, methinks, have been ready to sacrifice what little enjoyment it might have planned for itself . . . if thereby the wintry blasts of our rude sphere might come tempered to such a man" (108). Such friction between spheres, however, does not always seem so accidental and indirect. In the case of Zenobia and Westervelt, for example, the conflict is an open one, for they "mutually repelled each other by some incompatibility of their spheres" (*CE* III, 150).

Nor does one have to be as unusual as Clifford or as alienated from one another as Zenobia and Westervelt in order to be aware of the ways in which one's own sphere differs from those of others. Holgrave differentiates himself from Phoebe when he tells her that "my own sphere does not so much lie among the flowers" (*CE* II, 93). As this example suggests, the problem of differing or even incompatible spheres need not be a disruptive one in Hawthorne's world. As a matter of fact, "it contributes greatly towards a man's moral and intellectual health, to be brought into habits of companionship with individuals unlike himself, who care little for his pursuits, and whose sphere and abilities he must go out of himself to appreciate" (*CE* I, 24). The real problems arise when the presence of others is felt not in the form of a sympathetic appreciation and acceptance of one's individualizing traits but in the form of a sinister attempt by another to impose his sphere on one's own. Even the self-centered Coverdale, his defenses weakened by illness, is vulnerable to such an invasion. "The spheres of our companions have, at such periods, a vastly greater influence upon our own, than when robust health gives us a repellent and self-defensive energy. Zenobia's sphere, I imagine, impressed powerfully on mine, and transformed me, during this period of my illness, into something like a mesmerical clairvoyant" (*CE* III, 46–47).

Zenobia, of course, is not interested in enchanting Coverdale; her primary concerns lie elsewhere, and he regains his individuality with his health. Priscilla, who is threatened in a similar way, is more vulnerable. She finds herself a "sad and lonely prisoner" (112) within the "sphere with which this dark, earthly magician had surrounded her" (201). And, as Coverdale notes, "when a young girl comes within the sphere of such a man, she is as perilously situated as the maiden whom, in old classical myths, the people used to expose to a dragon" (71), for "there are some spheres, the contact with which inevitably degrades the high, debases the pure and the beautiful" (101).

Hawthorne's characters seem especially threatened by any relationship that implies the "transfusion of one spirit into another" (*LL* I, 62). In the case of Westervelt and

Priscilla, the movement of one sphere toward another is not generated by a reciprocal sympathy that draws the two together without either losing its individuality and being swallowed up by the other. Rather the movement is initiated by a strong, detached curiosity on the part of one being concerning the selfhood of another. And this non-reciprocal, intellectual interest in the girl threatens her very existence, for, having been robbed of the power of centralizing the world, she becomes merely one of the "creatures and circumstances" forming the circumference of another's sphere.

Other people are not, however, the only disruptive threat to the stability of the interlocking spheres that form the chain of humanity; any one of the links may be instantly and irreparably broken by any "accident, misfortune, crime, or peculiarity of character, that puts an individual ajar with the world" (*CE* IV, 113). As we have seen, Hawthorne feels that in his own case a peculiar preference for solitude combines with "some witchcraft or other" to place him slightly apart from the "chain of human sympathy" (*CW* I, 317). In this sense he resembles Wakefield, whose fate it was "to retain his original shares of human sympathies, and to be still involved in human interests, while he had lost his reciprocal influence on them" (*CE* IX, 138). As a matter of fact, most of Hawthorne's major characters experience similar disruptions in their relations with the chain of humanity and find themselves in the position of having to create a new sphere for themselves.

For Hester Prynne, the Scarlet A takes "her out of the ordinary relations with humanity and [encloses] her in a sphere by herself" (*CE* I, 54).

In all her intercourse with society, however, there was nothing that made her feel as if she belonged to it. Every gesture, every word, and even the silence of those with whom she came in contact, implied, and often expressed, that she was banished, as much alone as if she inhabited another sphere, or communicated with the common nature by other organs and senses than the rest of human kind. She stood apart from mortal interests, yet close beside them, like a ghost that revisits the familiar fireside, and can no longer make itself seen or felt; no more smile with the household joy, nor mourn with the kindred sorrow; or, should it succeed in manifesting its forbidden sympathy, awakening only terror and horrible repugnance. [84]

Hester, along with Pearl, stands in a wide "circle of seclusion from human society" (94), and the force which separates them from the community, like death itself, imposes an unbridgeable gap between two realms so incompatible that the sympathy generated in one produces "terror and repugnance" in the other. Like a ghost, Hester moves through the community and finds everything she wishes to touch "remote from her own sphere, and utterly beyond her reach" (239).

Hester, therefore, "with wild and ghostly scenery all around her" (116) "casts away the fragments of a broken chain" (168) which had once formed the circumference of her world and patiently waits seven years for an opportunity to construct a new surrounding reality. Finally, in the enchanted sunshine of the forest she seems to accomplish her purpose, for she and Dimmesdale come to feel themselves "inhabitants of the same sphere" (190). In making a new sphere for herself, however, Hester radically alters the structure of the world in which Pearl has lived for seven years; "another inmate had been admitted within the circle of her mother's feelings, and so modified the aspect of them all, that Pearl, the returning wanderer, could not find her wonted place, and hardly knew where she was" (208). She seems to have "strayed out of the sphere in which she and her mother dwelt together, and was now seeking vainly to return to it" (208). In order to readmit Pearl to her world, Hester must resume the Scarlet A and with it her old relation to society.

Miriam Schafer, who resembles Hester in several ways, makes a similar attempt to establish a new life. Miriam, however, is not oppressed by the heavy atmosphere of Puritan New England. In the "enchanted air" of Rome, "land of Art," she is in a better position to escape the burden of a sinful past. "I had made for myself a new sphere, and found new friends, new occupations, new hopes, and enjoyments. My heart, methinks, was almost as unburthened, as if there had been no miserable life behind me" (96). Nevertheless, the boundaries of her new life are shattered by the shadow of the past cast by the substantial figure of her model, and she is forced to seek other means of constructing a new life.

Together with Donatello, who loves her, she commits a crime that seems to circumscribe a new sphere capable of resisting not only the thrust of the intrusive past but that of the present as well.

Their deed—the crime which Donatello wrought, and Miriam accepted on the instant—had wreathed itself, as she said, like a serpent, in inextricable links about both their souls, and drew them into one, by its terrible contractile power. . . . So intimate, in those first moments, was the union, that it seemed as if their new sympathy annihilated all other ties, and that they were released from the chain of humanity; a new sphere, a special law, had been created for them alone. The world could not come near them; they were safe! [*CE* IV, 174]

This intimate circle like the one that momentarily surrounded Hester and Dimmesdale is formed by a strange sympathy generated by a mutual crime and is not a lasting one. The movement of sympathy which circumscribes it is interrupted when Donatello, overwhelmed by a growing realization of the horror of his crime, imposes a barrier between himself and Miriam's "tenderness and devotion" (198). "He . . . looked at Miriam with strangely half-awakened and bewildered eyes, when she sought to bring his mind into sympathy with hers, and so relieve his heart of the burden that lay lumpishly upon it" (197). Miriam, consequently, like Wakefield, Hester, and Hawthorne himself, finds herself without a reciprocal relationship with the world—"I pity him from the depths of my soul! As for myself, I am past my own or others' pity" (199)—standing forever on the "other side of a fathomless abyss" doomed to remain within the "sepulchral gloom" (462) of her isolation.

This horrifying experience is not, however, limited to the perverse and dark characters in Hawthorne's world. One does not have to be directly involved in the disruptive crime, accident, or misfortune in order to have one's sphere threatened by it. Miriam's friend Hilda seems at first to enjoy an ontological security which sets her apart from everyone else; "keeping a maiden heart within her bosom, she rejoiced in the freedom that enabled her still to choose her own sphere, and dwell in it, if she pleased, without another inmate" (328). Not only is Hilda free to select her own surrounding reality (a luxury most of Hawthorne's characters do not enjoy), but she also is able to resist the influence of uncongenial spheres: "There was a certain simplicity that made everyone her friend, but it was combined with a subtle attribute of reserve, that insensibly kept those at a distance who were not suited to her sphere" (63). Nevertheless the stability of her world is severely threatened when she witnesses Miriam and Donatello's crime. The freedom that has allowed her to enjoy a self-sufficient privacy vanishes and with it the ability to regulate her relations with others by means of an instinctive simplicity. Now she finds herself—as so many of Hawthorne's characters do—caught in a tension between distance and desire. On the one hand, she acknowledges the necessity for maintaining the distance the crime has imposed between herself and Miriam because Miriam's "powerful magnetism would be too much for [her]" (208) to resist, while, on the other, the terrible secret she holds "imprisoned in [her] heart" generates a "great need of sympathy" (342–343). Hilda, in other words, suddenly both needs and fears others, and there seems little hope that she will be able to resolve the tension between the two contradictory impulses.

Fortunately, however, Hilda has unconsciously asserted a marvelous influence on Kenyon: "the idea of this girl . . . had modified the whole sphere in which Kenyon had his being" (409), and he is led, therefore, "to shape his own movements so as to bring him often within her sphere" (99). The happy result of his persistence is that Hilda falls in love with him and gains the sympathy she so deeply needs.

The motif of the sphere, then, embodies the basic intersubjective tension which torments Hawthorne's characters.

At the same time that it expresses that sense of privacy and separateness which is such an important aspect of the characters' lives, it also points to the fact that "our souls after all are not our own. We convey a property in them to those with whom we associate, but to what extent can never be known, until we feel the tug, the agony of our abortive effort to resume an exclusive sway over ourselves" (*CE* III, 194). That effort, of course, is a central theme in Hawthorne's writing, and the motif that most often signals its appearance is that of the gaze.

As we have seen, Hawthorne's characters find themselves in a threatening world where the primary danger comes from the gaze of other people. One expression of that danger is the "witchcraft of the Maule's eye" (*CE* II, 189) which allows the carpenter to "look into people's minds" and to "send them, if he pleased, to do errands to his grandfather, in the spiritual world" (189–190). All of the Maules, including Holgrave, recognize the power of the gaze and use it against others before others can employ it against them. This is the meaning of Holgrave's story of Alice Pyncheon. She seals her fate when she casts an "admiring glance" (201) at Matthew Maule, for he recognizes the threat her gaze poses to his own subjectivity: " 'Does the girl look at me as if I were a brute beast?' thought he, setting his teeth. 'She shall know whether I have a human spirit, and the worse for her if it prove stronger than her own' " (201). Because his will is stronger, he drains Alice of her inwardness in the same way she has unconsciously threatened his.

Such a situation is a common one in Hawthorne's world. His characters are haunted by the fear that their "interests are in control of individuals who neither love nor understand [them]" (*CE* I, 40). Like Hepzibah Pyncheon, they isolate themselves out of fear of the "public eye" (*CE* II, 39). She realizes that once she appears before others, "strange and unloving eyes should have the privilege of gazing" (46). And to be the object of the unloving gaze of the other is to be in his power.

For some reason or other, not very easy to analyze, there had hardly been so bitter a pang in all her previous misery about the matter, as what thrilled Hepzibah's heart, on overhearing the above conversation [between two working men outside her cent shop]. The testimony in regard to her scowl was frightfully important; it seemed to hold up her image, wholly relieved from the false light of her self-partialities, and so hideous that she dared not look at it. She was absurdly hurt, moreover, by the slight and idle effect that her setting-up shop—an event of such breathless interest to herself—appeared to have upon the public, of which these two men were the nearest representatives. A glance; a passing word or two; a coarse laugh. . . . They cared nothing for her dignity, and just as little for her degradation. [48]

The two laboring men rob the aristocratic woman of a part of her being. Without access to or concern with her inwardness they conclude that she scowls out of "pure ugliness of temper" (47); and Hepzibah, confronted by her image in a world not made by her, feels her life begin to drain out of her. In the world's eye she is no more than one of the figures on the wandering boy's barrel organ, a mere mechanism performing a recognizable role in society's play. Like her brother Clifford, she fears to leave the protective darkness of the old house, because she is afraid that she will become a "figure such as one sometimes imagines himself to be, with the world's eyes upon him, in a troubled dream" (275).[4]

Hester Prynne is also burdened by the "heavy weight of a thousand unrelenting eyes, all fastened upon her" (*CE* I, 57), by the "intense consciousness of being the object of severe and universal observation" (60). For her, both the "gaze of a new eye" and the "cold stare of familiarity" (85–86) are equally intolerable. In both cases, she is forced to the recognition that she exists for others as an object to be looked at and judged. This is an especially frightening experience for her because it robs her of the one positive result of the Scarlet A, her freedom. If she is caught by the gaze of others and fixed in their world, she will be deprived of her painfully acquired power of objective judgment, a power which derives from the "estranged point of view" from which she views human institutions and which allows her to criticize all of them with "hardly more reverence than the Indian would feel for the clerical band, the judicial robe, the pillory, the gallows, the fireside, or the church" (199).

Hester, however, does not passively surrender to the gaze of others. She seeks to control and distort their perception

---

[4] Her experience parallels that of the old man in *The Dolliver Romance:* "He longed to be gazed at by the loving eyes now closed; he shrank from the hard stare of them that loved him not. Walking the streets seldom and reluctantly, he felt a dreary impulse to elude the people's observation, as if with a sense that he had gone irrevocably out of fashion, and broken his connecting links with the network of human life; or else it was that nightmare-feeling which we sometimes have in dreams, when we seem to find ourselves wandering through a crowded avenue, with the noonday sun upon us, in some wild extravagance of dress or nudity" (*CW* XI, 32).

of her. The "studied austerity of her dress," the "lack of demonstration in her manners" (163), her decision "to hold intercourse with her fellow creatures" only in "gloomy twilight"—"It was only the darkened house which could contain her" (161)—are all indications of Hester's refusal to be defined by others. She affirms her autonomy by forcing the public to accept an exterior and superficial view of her which she herself is instrumental in forming. Her true identity, carefully hidden behind the public mask, emerges at last in a "flood of sunshine" (199) when, after seven years, she encounters Dimmesdale in the forest. But at this moment she discovers the painful limits to her freedom through Pearl, who insists that Hester permanently retain the Scarlet A and confining cap which have shaped her image in the public eye. The freedom generated by her estranged point of view is incompatible with her devotion to her daughter and with her dream of possessing a "home and fireside of our own" (212) where Pearl will sit upon Dimmesdale's knee. Insofar as she clings to this social ideal, she retains her membership in society, a relation which precludes the possibility that she can dissociate completely her personal identity from its manifestation to the world. In this sense her predicament is precisely Hawthorne's. As we shall see, he too is acutely sensitive to the dangers of the gaze but cannot consent to renounce once and for all his claims to society. But while Hester in the end can only passively accept her predicament and serve as a counselor to others, Hawthorne looks to literature as a way to hold on to certain advantages that come from being with others at the same time that he asserts his personal autonomy.

His attempt to accomplish this goal is the subject of most

of his first-person narratives, where he examines the theme of looking from the point of view of the watcher rather than from that of the victim who has his sovereignty over himself stolen away. As many commentators have noticed, Coverdale of *The Blithedale Romance* seeks access to the secrets of others without giving them access to his own. He puts Hollingsworth "under [a] microscope" (*CE* III, 69), "peep[s] beneath [Priscilla's] folded petals" (125), and tries to seek out the mystery of Zenobia's life.

"Mr. Coverdale," said she [Zenobia], one day, as she saw me watching her, while she arranged my gruel on the table, "I have been exposed to a great deal of eye-shot in the few years of my mixing in the world, but never, I think, to precisely such glances as you are in the habit of favoring me with. I seem to interest you very much; and yet—or else a woman's instinct is for once deceived—I cannot reckon you an admirer. What are you seeking to discover in me?"

"The mystery of your life," answered I, surprised into the truth by the unexpectedness of her attack. "And you will never tell me."

She bent her head towards me, and let me look into her eyes, as if challenging me to draw a plummet-line into the depth of her consciousness.

"I see nothing now," said I, closing my own eyes, "unless it be the face of a sprite, laughing at me from the bottom of a deep well." [47–48]

This passage is an important one, for it expresses subtly and completely the tension in Hawthorne's world between knowledge of others and self-knowledge. As a self-confessed peeper and pryer Coverdale is Hawthorne's most complex dramatization of the Paul Pry figure and the problem he encounters in attempting to achieve that impossible ideal of being "unseen of men . . . even while standing in their eyes" (*CE* III, 188). Coverdale, of course, fears relationship because he associates it with loss of identity—he speaks of the importance of keeping his individuality "inviolate" (99)—and yet, as his narrative makes clear, he feels empty and incomplete without others and longs to be together with them. But he cannot be separate from and attached to others at the same time. He can, however, express his fascination with others; he can be a voyeur.[5]

As Coverdale's encounter with Zenobia suggests, however, the position of the voyeur is a problematic one. He seeks to catch the other at an unguarded and intimate moment, a moment when the other will be naked and available to his concealed gaze. For the voyeur desires access to the solitariness of the other. He wishes to experience from the outside another's life as it is lived from the inside. This is one explanation for his dependence on the visual sense. Sight is the sense of the passive observer. I can look at things and still remain at rest, watching from a distance. They are present to me, but I am not drawn into their presence.[6]

This distance, of course, is necessary to the realization of the voyeur's desire, for his success depends on his remaining outside the knowledge of those whom he watches. He values their innocence because it guarantees him his sovereignty. They must not know that they have become the

[5] I am indebted here to R. D. Laing's discussion of a voyeuristic situation in *Self and Others* (New York: Pantheon Books, 1968), p. 104.

[6] For a helpful discussion of the relation between sight and distance see Hans Jonas, "The Nobility of Sight," in *The Phenomenon of Life* (New York: Dell, 1966), pp. 135–156.

objects of the desires of a hidden other, for then they will call him to account, force him to justify himself and to admit that he has his foundation outside himself. This situation the voyeur, like Sartre's man at the keyhole, seeks to avoid by becoming a "pure consciousness of things,"[7] or, as Coverdale puts it, by melting "into a scene as a wreath of vapor melts into a larger cloud" (*CE* III, 207). Otherwise he will be caught as Coverdale is by Zenobia, surprised into truth, and forced into an eye-to-eye encounter. Once this occurs his desires are forever thwarted. Once Zenobia becomes aware of Coverdale's probing look she shields herself against it by offering him her own eyes, for she knows that all he will be able to see there is a demeaning and mocking reflection of himself.

Unhappily for his peace of mind, the voyeur cannot remain hidden. Even though he distances himself, he is as caught and as fascinated by the spectacle that lies before him as Alice Pyncheon is by the eyes of Matthew Maule. Coverdale, for example, is so "transfixed" (157) by the events he witnesses from his hotel window that he is detected and recognized at "his post of observation" (158). The voyeur, it seems, cannot escape the dangers involved in looking and being seen. Enchanted by the spectacle before him, he resembles in his rigidity Lot and his company or the victims of the head of Medusa.[8] And once he is immobilized he becomes accessible to others and is disen-

---

[7] Sartre, *Being and Nothingness*, p. 235.

[8] For a discussion of the relation between looking and the idea of being turned to stone, as well as for a Freudian reading of the situation of the voyeur see Otto Fenichel, "The Scoptophilic Instinct and Identification," *The Collected Papers of Otto Fenichel* (New York: Norton, 1953), pp. 373–397.

chanted by their accusing eyes. The voyeur, apparently, is doomed always to become the victim of the person he watches.

This certainly is a central issue in *The Blithedale Romance*. As a voyeur Coverdale is pathetically unsuccessful. He constantly exposes himself to his friends, and the harder he tries to direct the reader's gaze toward others the more persistently it focuses on him. But does this mean that Hawthorne's strategy also has failed? Perhaps he has called attention to Coverdale in order to divert it from himself in the same way that Coverdale sometimes prevents others from interrogating him by first unsettling them with his scrutiny and questions. Hawthorne's relationship to Coverdale may parallel that of the narrator of "Sketches from Memory" to the Englishman whom he sees taking notes in the cabin of a canal boat.

Perceiving that the Englishman was taking notes in a memorandum-book, with occasional glances round the cabin, I presumed that we were all to figure in a future volume of travels, and amused my ill-humor by falling into the probable vein of his remarks. He would hold up an imaginary mirror, wherein our reflected faces would appear ugly and ridiculous, yet still retain an undeniable likeness to the originals. Then, with more sweeping malice, he would make these caricatures the representatives of great classes of my countrymen.

He glanced at the Virginia schoolmaster, a Yankee by birth, who, to recreate himself, was examining a freshman from Schenectady College in the conjugation of a Greek verb. Him, the Englishman would portray as the scholar of America, and compare his erudition to a schoolboy's Latin theme, made up of scraps, ill selected and worse put together. . . . He lifted his eye-glass to inspect a western lady, who at once became aware of the glance, reddened, and retired deeper into the female part of the cabin. Here was the pure, modest, sensitive, and shrinking woman of America,—shrinking when no evil is intended, and sensitive like diseased flesh, that thrills if you but point at it; and strangely modest, without confidence in the modesty of other people; and admirably pure, with such a quick apprehension of all impurity.

In this manner I went through all the cabin, hitting everybody as hard a lash as I could, and laying the whole blame on the infernal Englishman. At length I caught the eyes of my own image in the looking-glass, where a number of the party were likewise reflected, and among them the Englishman, who, at that moment was intently observing myself. [*CE* X, 434–435]

This text expresses nicely the sly and yet threatening manner in which consciousnesses approach one another in Hawthorne's world. The narrator is first aware of himself as a member of a group that is being scrutinized by the unloving eyes of an alien and defined and categorized in a cruelly perverse way. The narrator meets this threat by removing, in his case, the constituent power of the gaze. This he accomplishes, interestingly, through an act of imaginative identification. By viewing his fellow travelers through the Englishman's eyes he avoids being himself the self-conscious object of the gaze. Even more. Not only is he now in the position of secure watcher, he does not even have to bear the burden of the knowledge that such a position is a violation of the sanctity of the human heart. The Englishman has become his surrogate, and through him he can participate innocently and safely in the secret process of watching and judging.

The glance into the mirror, however, destroys the authenticity of such a mystified vision. For the sense of identification disappears the moment the narrator realizes that his point of view is limited by his body—and that realization comes when he catches the eyes of his own image in the mirror—which also makes him available to others. The problem, in short, is precisely one of visibility. Because man has a body he must sooner or later "stand revealed in [his] proper individuality" (*CE* II, 40). He yearns, of course, as Hepzibah Pyncheon does, to be "unseen" like a "disembodied divinity" (40), a condition that would allow him to watch others without being seen himself. Consequently, the narrator of "Sketches from Memory" seeks to use the protecting cover of darkness to prevent a recurrence of his disconcerting experience with the Englishman.

My head was close to the crimson curtain,—the sexual division of the boat,—behind which I continually heard whispers and stealthy footsteps; the noise of a comb laid on the table, or a slipper dropt on the floor; the twang, like a broken harp-string, caused by loosening a tight belt; the rustling of a gown in its descent; and the unlacing of a pair of stays. My ear seemed to have the properties of an eye; a visible image pestered my fancy in the darkness; the curtain was withdrawn between me and the western lady, who yet disrobed herself without a blush. [*CE* X, 435–436]

Here, apparently, is a solution to the narrator's problem. Protected by darkness from the inquisitive eyes of others, he is able to study the western lady with an intensity which validates her worst fears but of which she is totally unaware. Here there is no danger that another transcending view will give his acts an objectivity that renders them subject to value judgments. Unfortunately, however, the burden of the body once again manifests itself: "Finally all was hushed in that quarter. Still, I was more broad awake than through the whole preceding day, and felt a feverish impulse to toss my limbs miles apart, and appease the unquietness of mind by that of matter. Forgetting that my berth was hardly as wide as a coffin, I turned suddenly over, and fell like an avalanche on the floor, to the disturbance of the whole community of sleepers" (436). Even under the cover of darkness and aided by the creative powers of the imagination man cannot achieve the privileges of "disembodied divinity." The body intrudes itself in the form of sexual desire with the result that the narrator is moved from the position of subject to that of object. His body, as it falls from the coffinlike bed, affirms its relation to those other falling objects, the comb, the slipper, the gown.

It appears, then, that for Hawthorne because man has a body there is no way he can escape from being in relation to others as others are in relation to him. Still, the heavy metaphorical weight clothing carries for Hawthorne implies that there are ways in which man can throw a "cloud over [his] transparency" (*CE* IV, 250). He can, as Father Hooper does, impose a veil between himself and the world. The veil, of course, does not conceal completely, but it does render ordinary human relations ambiguous and gives its wearer certain advantages over those who remain unveiled. Father Hooper, for example, after veiling himself, seems able to penetrate more deeply into the minds and hearts of his congregation: "Each member of the congregation, the most innocent girl, and the man of hardened breast, felt as if the preacher had crept upon them, behind his awful veil, and discovered their hoarded iniquity of deed or thought" (*CE* IX, 40). Father Hooper's "piece of crepe" is, of course, the sign of the "mystery" (52) which governs all human relationships. Most of Hawthorne's characters veil themselves in one way or another albeit without inspiring the dread that the minister does. Holgrave, for example, "habitually masked whatever lay near his heart" by his "New England reserve" (*CE* II, 301), and Zenobia's pseudonymity is "a sort of mask in which she comes before the world, retaining all the privileges of privacy—a contrivance . . . like the white drapery of the Veiled Lady, only a little more transparent" (*CE* III, 8). In short, any aspect of self that is "meant for the world's eye . . . is therefore a veil and concealment" (*CE* III, 149).

Hawthorne, of course, is as fond of veils as are his characters. His fascination with pseudonyms is well known—he used at different times M. de l'Aubépine, Oberon, and Ashley Allen Royce—and he published many of his early sketches either anonymously or under the signature of Nathaniel Hawthorne, having inserted a "w" in his family name during his last year at college.[9] Fiction for him is a way of "opening an intercourse with the world" (*CE* IX, 6) only in the sense that it is an appeal to "sensibilities . . . such as are diffused among us all. So far as I am a man of really individual attributes, I veil my face; nor am I . . . one of those supremely hospitable people, who serve up their own hearts delicately fried, with brain sauce, as a tidbit for their beloved public" (*CE* X, 33). Hence in "The Custom House" he writes that "we may prate of circumstances that lie around us, and even of ourself, but still keep the inmost Me behind its veil" (*CE* I, 4). In other words,

<hr/>

[9] Moncure D. Conway, *Life of Nathaniel Hawthorne* (London: Walter Scott, 1895), p. 89.

he conceives of the act of writing as a way of maintaining a privileged point of view. His fiction, he implies, like the white drapery of the Veiled Lady, will "endow [him] with many of the privileges of a disembodied spirit"' (CE III, 6).

Veils, however, are curious coverings that reveal as well as conceal and as such suggest a hidden connection between secrecy and self-revelation, a connection that for Hawthorne characterizes the social. Consequently, there are times when the self-protective veil seems to hold its wearer in a "bondage which is worse . . . than death" (CE III, 112–113). This is a bondage to which man as a social being is condemned. There is one way, however, in which he can escape: by forming an extra-social relation with one other person, the relation of love. Love, for Hawthorne, is a form of fascination that has the effect of removing the lover and beloved from their social matrix and placing them in a world of their own. As such it is a force which a writer must investigate in detail.

3

The Enchantment of Love

Romantic love . . . is characterized by its simultaneously possessing these two ingredients: a feeling of being "enchanted" by another being who produces complete "illusion" in us, and a feeling of being absorbed by him to the core of our being, as if he had torn us from our own vital depths and we were living transplanted, our vital roots within him. Another way of saying this is that a person in love feels himself totally surrendered to the one he loves.

José Ortega y Gasset, *On Love*

Hawthorne's response to other people is controlled by his desire to protect the frontiers of his selfhood from trespass by another person. So basic is this self-protective impulse in his world that there is only one occasion when it fails to operate: when one person becomes fascinated by another and falls in love. The power of love is so overwhelming that it does not simply neutralize the strategies protecting the individual's inwardness from the curious attention of others; it manifests itself as a desire that can only be satisfied by the fusion of two individualities. "Are we singular or plural, dearest? Has not each of us a right to use the first person singular, when speaking in behalf of our united being?" (*LL* I, 64), Hawthorne writes to Sophia. So "intimate" is their "communion" (108) that he is led to confess, "I am only myself when thou art within my reach" (*LL* II, 186). Now that another person is "intertwined with [his] being" (200), his earlier yearning for seclusion is replaced by a desire for a "solitude of a united two" (I, 213–214).

To speak in this way, of course, is to acknowledge one's absolute dependence on the existence of another person, to recognize the presence of an other at the center of oneself. Of this Hawthorne is well aware. The *Love Letters* are a record of his conviction that Sophia makes him be. "Nothing else is real, except the bond between thee and me," he writes to her. "The people around me are but shadows. I am myself but a shadow, till thou takest me in thy arms, and convertest me into substance" (II, 256). "Indeed, we are but shadows," he insists in another letter, "we are not endowed with real life, and all that seems most real about us is but the thinnest substance of a dream—till the heart is touched. That touch creates us—then we begin to be." (I, 225).

Love, it seems, is a remarkable power that frees man from the uneasiness and shame he normally feels in the presence of another. In this case the transformation of shadow into substance is a positive rather than a threatening act. Unlike the narrator of "Sketches from Memory" when he finds himself the object of the Englishman's gaze, the beloved need not fear that the lover will make him the object of a series of value judgments. Sophia reveals to Hawthorne what he is, but that revelation is not experienced as the imposition of an objectifying meaning from the outside. Just the reverse is true. Her eyes and touch are not ones that solidify and immobilize thereby making him feel he is no more than one object among others. They convert shadow into substance, but that transformation is in the form of an incarnating act that frees rather than imprisons. It is Sophia's "magic touch" (II, 35) that removes the "viewless bolts and bars" of the "haunted chamber" in which Hawthorne spends his "lonely youth" (I, 223), releasing him from a world of shadows and making him conscious of "something real" (121). In converting his shadowy life into substance Sophia provides Hawthorne at last with a secure identity and makes it possible for him to live a normal life among others.

Sophia, in effect, becomes the foundation and support of

Hawthorne's selfhood, a function traditionally served by God. And Hawthorne, in describing that relationship, uses the familiar religious language of conversion.

Whenever I return to Salem, I feel how dark my life would be, without the light thou shedst upon it—how cold, without the warmth of thy love. Sitting in this chamber, where my youth wasted itself in vain, I can partly estimate the change that has been wrought. It seems as if the better part of me has been born, since then. I had walked those many years in darkness, and might so have walked through life, with only a dreamy notion that there was any light in the universe, if thou hadst not kissed my eyelids, and given me to see.   [I, 236]

This passage suggests the transcendent power love possesses for Hawthorne and explains why his fictional characters so often see the persons they love as gods and goddesses and attribute to them divine powers.[1] In the *Love Letters* and the fiction the effect of love resembles that of a religious experience: it transforms both the lover and the world around him.

And it was in this hour, so full of doubt and awe, that the one miracle was wrought, without which every human existence is a blank. The bliss, which makes all things true, beautiful, and

---

[1] This is a characteristic Hawthorne shares with a number of other nineteenth-century novelists, and according to J. Hillis Miller, is one that suggests that love is "displaced religious desire, a search for a divine foundation for the self in another person." Victorian fiction, he argues, "may be said to have as its fundamental theme an exploration of the various ways in which a man may seek to make a god of another person in a world without God, or at any rate in a world where the traditional ways in which the self may be related to God no longer seem open" (*The Form of Victorian Fiction* [Notre Dame: University of Notre Dame Press, 1968], pp. 100, 96).

holy, shone around this youth and maiden. They were conscious of nothing sad nor old. They transfigured the earth, and
made it Eden again, and themselves the two first dwellers in it.
The dead man, so close beside them, was forgotten. At such a
crisis, there is no Death; for Immortality is revealed anew, and
embraces everything in its hallowed atmosphere.   [*CE* II, 307]

Like Hawthorne in his lonely chamber, Holgrave has just
a moment before been surrounded by a "shapeless gloom,
which [he] must mould into gloomy shapes" (*CE* II, 306).
But now in an instant the "black moment" is transformed
into a "blissful one" when "hope, warmth, and joy" (306)
enter the dismal house with Phoebe. From an overwhelming
sense of guilt and retribution to a feeling of everlasting
youthfulness—this is the change love effects in Holgrave;
and the effect on the external world is equally impressive.
What was once dark and threatening is now bright and
promising, a transfiguration remarkably similar to the one
wrought in Hawthorne's world by his marriage to Sophia.
"It is as if the original relation between Man and Nature
were restored in my case, and that I were to look exclusively to her for the support of my Eve and myself. . . .
The fight with the world—the struggle of a man among
men—the agony of the universal effort to wrench the means
of life from a host of greedy competitors—all this seems like
a dream to me. My business is merely to live and to enjoy;
and whatever is essential to life and enjoyment will come
as naturally as the dew from Heaven" (*CE* VIII, 332). For
both Holgrave and Hawthorne love offers a release from
the burden of living alone in a "haunted chamber," because
it joins them to another person who will sustain and guide
them. Reality now seems the result of a benevolent intent

and, consequently, existence is no longer felt as a burden that must be supported by one's own exertions. The "new love makes the old earth seem so happy and glorious a place, that not a thousand years can exhaust it" (*CW* XI, 404).

Unhappily, however, in Hawthorne's fiction not all love transformations are so long-lasting. The idyllic vision of the *Love Letters* is not always reflected in the experiences of his characters. Hester and Dimmesdale, for example, share a remarkable transfiguration in their world, but in their case it is one that does not last. Meeting alone for the first time in seven years, they suddenly find themselves surrounded by the plenitude of an unfallen Eden. "And, as if the gloom of earth and sky had been but the effluence of these two mortal hearts, it vanished with their sorrow. All at once, as with a sudden smile of heaven, forth burst the sunshine, pouring a very flood into the obscure forest, gladdening each green leaf, transmuting the yellow fallen ones to gold, and gleaming adown the gray trunks of the solemn trees" (*CE* I, 202–203). " 'Do I feel joy again,' " asks Dimmesdale. " 'Methought the germ of it was dead in me! O Hester, thou art my better angel! I seem to have flung myself—sick, sin-stained, and sorrow-blackened—down upon these forest-leaves, and to have risen up all made anew' " (201–202). In the case of these lovers, of course, the conversion is premature and love's Eden a mirage, both the result of a mystification created by the subversive power of Hester's will. As she will become painfully aware, for them as for Septimius Felton and Rose Garfield "love was the illusive state and the estrangement the real truth, the disenchanted verity" (*CW* XI, 297).

The disappearance of Hester's and Dimmesdale's forest

Eden, of course, puts into question the reality of all such happy places. To be sure, not all of Hawthorne's happy lovers find themselves estranged as Hester and Dimmesdale are; but the power of love in all other cases as in theirs is a form of enchantment. The transfiguration of self and world that occurs is generated by the lover's fascination. The beloved is a "mighty enchantress" (*LL* II, 69) who weaves "love's web of sorcery" (*CE* II, 319). The world of lovers consequently, like the realm of romance, is one that exists on the margin of the ordinary one, an artificial realm where the usual relation between dream and reality is reversed. The experience of living in such a world, "within the circle of a spell, a solitude in the midst of men" (*CE* II, 305), therefore, is only a momentary one, even for the occasional pair of happy lovers in Hawthorne's work. In the case of Phoebe and Holgrave, for example, the "heavy earth dream settles down again" (307), and they are forced to leave their paradise to go out and "meet the world" (307).

Nevertheless in their case a permanent transformation seems to have taken place. Holgrave no longer sees the world in the same way. Suddenly he is able to "conform myself to laws, and the peaceful practice of society" (307). Although no real change has occurred in the social structure, Holgrave now assumes that he can live safely, even happily, within its confines. The real world to which Hester Prynne returns from the enchanted forest eventually reveals the magical moment to be a mocking "delusion" (*CE* I, 240), but for Holgrave, the real and enchanted realms seem continuous. He returns to the world but no longer feels the burden of materiality, for his existence is not felt as a weight he must support. Unlike Hester, he does not have to look at the world directly but can study its reflection in the magical mirror of the beloved. Consequently, it is experienced as ordered and significant, for the beloved like God both sustains and directs. Hence Holgrave is not affected by the problems that burden other people. He projects on society at large the light of his own happiness with the result that everything seems lovely and charming. His vision dominates the final pages of *The House of the Seven Gables.* Uncle Venner's "farm" is replaced by a "gingerbread" (*CE* II, 317) cottage; the House of the Seven Gables is abandoned for a fine "country-house," an "excellent . . . piece of domestic architecture" (314), and even the demeaning activities of getting and spending seem glorified when Hepzibah, after keeping a cent shop for three months, "rides off in her carriage with a couple of hundred thousand" (318). No doubt these incredible (and ironic) transformations were in Hawthorne's mind when he wrote Evert Duyckinck that he intended to bring the book to a "prosperous close.[2] Needless to say, in a novel that portrays society as dedicated to the "sordid accumulation of copper coin" (81), a prosperous ending is not necessarily a happy one. Holgrave and Phoebe, after all, do not build their dream house. They merely move from one constructed by Colonel Pyncheon into one built by his descendant, the Judge, in effect trading in an old ghost for a new one.

Love, then, does not solve the problems posed in *The House of the Seven Gables,* but it smooths them away much as it does at the end of *The Marble Faun.*[3] Here again love

[2] Quoted by Eleanor Melville Metcalf, *Herman Melville: Cycle and Epicycle* (Cambridge: Harvard University Press, 1953), p. 103.

[3] In *Septimius Felton,* describing the effect of Rose on Septimius'

is given a divine dimension. Hilda, when she decides to marry Kenyon, abandons the "virgin's shrine" and comes "down from her old tower, to be herself enshrined and worshipped as a household Saint, in the light of her husband's fireside" (*CE* IV, 461). But just as the "miracle" of love can offer no real cure for the "energy of disease" (*CE* II, 23) that controls human relationships in *The House of the Seven Gables*, so in *The Marble Faun* it can provide no solution to the novel's central problem, determining the meaning of Donatello's adventures. Hilda rejects the two possible interpretations of the young Italian's life that Kenyon offers and forces the sculptor finally to abandon his interpretive quest altogether, to face the meaninglessness of his exiled condition, and to look to her to provide a direction for his life. "But the mind wanders wild and wide; and, so lonely as I live and work, I have neither pole-star above, nor light of cottage-windows here below, to bring me home. Were you my guide, my counsellor, my inmost friend, with that white wisdom which clothes you as with a celestial garment, all would go well. Oh, Hilda, guide me home" (*CE* IV, 460–461).

For Kenyon, as for Holgrave, a "black moment" is transformed into a "blissful one" by the power of love. Suddenly the world seems full of "human promise" (*CE* IV, 461), and so, with plans to return to his "own land" (461), he simply turns his back on the problem of the meaning of

---

troubled mind, Hawthorne writes: "She reconciled him, in some secret way, to life as it was, to imperfection, to decay; without any help from her intellect, but through the influence of her character, she seemed, not to solve, but to smooth away, problems that troubled him; merely by being, by womanhood, by simplicity, she interpreted God's ways to him" (*CW*, XI, 287–288).

Donatello's adventures. Safe on their own shores, the lovers presumably will live unbothered by the troubles that have plagued them in Rome and, one supposes, will continue to burden other people. The narrator, however, puts the lovers' future happiness into question when he introduces the possibility that on their return to America they may discover their "native air has lost its invigorating quality, and that life has shifted its reality to the spot where [they] have deemed [themselves] only temporary residents" (461). In other words, the ideal of a *home*, a "house and moderate garden spot of one's own" (*CE* II, 156) may be as much an ideal out of reach, as much "beyond the scope of man's actual possession" (*CE* IV, 73) as is the possibility of an unequivocal interpretation of Donatello's adventures.

Still, the happiness of the united lovers remains impervious to the narrator's subversive doubts, for the effect of their love is to set them apart from the world in which he remains an exile. They live as if there were two worlds with "different but permeable dimensions."[4] Falling in love confers on their lives the semblance of a beginning and a continuity that removes them from the world they previously

---

[4] José Ortega y Gasset, *On Love*, trans. Toby Talbot (Cleveland: World, 1957), pp. 66–67. "This is the common 'state of grace' of the lover and the mystic," Ortega continues. "They are not affected by this life and this world; for better or for worse, such things no longer matter to them. In our normal situation, things which we do and suffer affect our innermost being, become problems for us, cause us anxiety, and harass us. For that reason we feel our existence as a weight painfully supported by our own strength. But if we move that inner nucleus to another region or another person outside the world, what happens then is that we lose our hold upon it and it remains suspended, as it were, in mid-air. As we pass through the real world we feel ourselves impregnable" (66).

have inhabited, a world ruled by the destructive powers of time. In both *The House of the Seven Gables* and *The Marble Faun* the present suffers under the burden of an oppressive and destructive past. The old Pyncheon house and the ruins of Rome are not so much symbols of human accomplishment and survival as they are ominous signs of man's mortality. For Holgrave the past is a reminder to man of the horror of his incarnation. It is "rotten" (*CE* II, 179): "it lies upon the present like a giant's dead body" (182) making old institutions seem "dead corpses" needing to be "buried" (179). In *The Marble Faun* material ruins always imply, often contain, decayed human ruins. Rome is a "sepulchral store-house of the past" (*CE* IV, 436), "a vast tomb" (74) containing a "long decaying corpse" (235). The forms of culture, in short, are as fragile as man himself, his memorials symbols of oblivion rather than a protection from it.

The nature of the relationship between the Edenic, timeless world of the lovers and the wholly material one that exists on its boundaries remains in the form of an unanswered question. Because the beginning of their love is the end of their story, the lovers never have to test the reality of the world they see reflected in each other's eyes against the destructive forces of time. That very fact, however, reminds the reader that they are literary lovers and implies that their union may be no more than a narrative convention. Such a suggestion, of course, opens a distance between the language of the novel and the empirical experience of the reader, between the realms of romance and reality. And once this distance is asserted, an important aspect of the relationship between the narrator and the happy lovers emerges. As we have seen, he questions the perceptions of the lovers who accept as reality the "hallowed atmosphere" created by their love and who plan to live their lives as if "this world were Heaven" (*CE* VIII, 334). In spite of such questioning, however, there is an important relationship between their vision and his own commitment of the creating of "an atmosphere of strange enchantment, beheld through which the inhabitants have a propriety of their own" (*CE* III, 2). The creative impulse is an expression of a longing for the home lovers seem to enjoy, but the narrator is never able to share their sense of a completed reality. Holgrave and Phoebe retreat to an "elegant country-seat" (*CE* II, 314) while the narrator is left with only a "castle in the air" (3); Kenyon and Hilda, filled with hope, return to their own land, while their "friend," the narrator, remains in exile to write their story.

The distance separating the lovers from the narrator like that setting their happiness apart from the problems that continue for the other characters is the sign of a conflict between private and social roles. Lovers are "bound . . . to each other" but "separated . . . from the world" (*CE* II, 305). Their relationship with each other is incompatible with the normal communal relations with others, a situation that means the creative power of love which has transfigured and renewed their world cannot be used to revitalize the larger community. That such a coincidence of private and social experiences is no more than a utopian dream is quite clear in *The Blithedale Romance*, a novel centrally concerned with the conflict between self-fulfillment and social obligation. At Blithedale love is not an insulating and protecting force that places man and woman "within the circle of a spell, a solitude in the midst of men" (*CE* II, 305). As a matter of fact, the Blithedale experiment may be seen as an attempt to substitute the power of "familiar love" (19) for the principle of accumulation that informs social institutions. The utopian enterprise seeks to free man from a prison of empty conventions, habits, and institutions which constitute the framework of society. By extending the boundaries of the idyllic world of lovers, so that relationship of love becomes a shared communal experience, the elaborate collection of mechanized and materialized rules that now govern human relationships will be left behind, and individuals will live together in a continuous and radical intimacy.

the footing, on which we all associated at Blithedale, was widely different from that of conventional society. While inclining us to the soft affections of the Golden Age, it seemed to authorize any individual, of either sex, to fall in love with any other, regardless of what would elsewhere be judged suitable and prudent. Accordingly, the tender passion was very rife among us, in various degrees of mildness or virulence, but mostly passing away with the state of things that had given it origin. This was all well enough; but, for a girl like Priscilla, and a woman like Zenobia, to jostle one another in their love of a man like Hollingsworth, was likely to be no child's play. [*CE* III, 72]

This "Arcadian freedom of falling in love" is the result of the destruction of those social forms that initially were designed to allow men to maintain the distance between each other that privacy requires but that have become the basis for the "false and cruel principles" (19) governing human relations in modern society. Once the members of the Blithedale community find themselves free of the "rusty iron frame-work" of a society designed to insure an independent, self-contained existence, they compulsively seek happiness in the form of other people with hardly any restraints at all. They are motivated, of course, by the utopian assumption that simply removing the obstacles that constitute the established system will allow the spontaneous commitment of one person to another that characterizes falling in love to become the founding principle of the community. But this attitude is no more than a dream. When human relationships are no longer controlled by "harmonious propriety" (73), they degenerate into an open conflict of individual desires fully as destructive as that generated by the mechanisms controlling the lives of the "outside barbarians" (20). The members of the Blithedale community seek intimacy with others, but, with one notable exception, they are all motivated by their own dreams and desires rather than by the discovery that their substance or reality is supplied by someone outside themselves.

Zenobia was in the door-way, not far from Hollingsworth. She gazed at Priscilla, in a very singular way. Indeed, it was a sight worth gazing at, and a beautiful sight too, as the fair girl sat at the feet of that dark, powerful figure. Her air, while perfectly modest, delicate, and virginlike, denoted her as swayed by Hollingsworth, attracted to him, and unconsciously seeking to rest upon his strength. I could not turn away my own eyes, but hoped that nobody, save Zenobia and myself, were witnessing this picture. [77]

This passage expresses clearly the tension between the social and the personal that informs *The Blithedale Romance*. Priscilla is spellbound by Hollingsworth. Her love for him takes the form of a fascination almost hypnotic in quality. Zenobia and Coverdale, in turn, seem as caught by the sight of the lovers as Priscilla is by Hollingsworth. Zenobia gazes intently at the lovers, and she is watched by Coverdale who is also watching the lovers. However, their interest in the lovers is no indication that the community is being renewed by the love born within it. Zenobia, who is herself attracted to Hollingsworth, seeks a way to break the enchantment that binds him to Priscilla; and Coverdale, although detached enough to recognize the implications of Zenobia's intense gaze, is hardly a disinterested, unembodied Paul Pry. As he later remarks, there is an "analogy . . . between Zenobia's situation and mine" (222). What these two watchers seek is not a way to share in the happiness the lovers seem to experience. Rather each desires to break the spell of love and to cast another in its place.

Normally the world of lovers is secure from such threats. Priscilla, after all, is not affected by Coverdale's "bitter honey" (76) when he hints that her image may not in fact be present in Hollingsworth's heart. Nor is she disturbed by Zenobia's moving condemnation of Hollingsworth's motives. "Her engrossing love made it all clear. Hollingsworth could have no fault. That was the one principle at the centre of the universe. And the doubtful guilt or possible integrity of other people, appearances, self-evident facts, the testimony of her own senses—even Hollingsworth's self-accusation, had he volunteered it—would have weighed not the value of a mote of thistle-down on the other side. So secure was she of his right, that she never thought of comparing it with another's wrong, but left the latter to himself" (220–221). As this passage suggests, love for Hawthorne, as for Ortega, is a phenomenon of attention.[5] The look that lovers exchange has a different structure from that that determines ordinary relationships. In the eyes of the lover the beloved is not one person among others who is judged in terms of some outside system of value. Rather the beloved is the foundation of all value, the person through whom the world will exist for the lover. When one falls in love there is an elimination of the people and things that previously have concerned him. His field of vision becomes progressively more narrow until it is filled by only one object. The lover's attention is so completely absorbed by one person that the rest of the world ceases to concern him; the beloved has dislodged and replaced it. It is in this sense that love can be understood as a form of hypnosis or enchantment. Priscilla is not disturbed by the eyes and judgments of others, for when lovers are "together [their] own world is round about [them] and all things else cease to exist" (*LL* II, 38–39). Her world can be threatened by only one catastrophe. "Hollingsworth's unkindness" (*CE* III, 242).

At first, however, Hollingsworth is ready to "sacrifice" (214) the girl who loves him, for his attention is as "fixed" on his philanthropic scheme as Priscilla's is on him. His mania, in effect, creates as abnormal an attention span as does her love. Prompted by Zenobia's promise to finance his scheme, he willingly hands Priscilla over to Westervelt and reclaims her only when he discovers that Zenobia probably will lose her fortune to her sister. Only the shock of Zenobia's death has the force to shatter his idea's exclusiveness in

[5] See Ortega, *On Love*, pp. 44–50.

such a way as to make a love relation possible. Prior to this point, he has been incapable of love, for, as Priscilla's devotion implies, love demands that consciousness be occupied by only one object. And even now he is incapable of loving in the same way that Holgrave and Kenyon are. In this novel love does not generate another world that completely removes the central characters from a problematical context. Even though he is "blest with the entire devotion of this one true heart, and [has] wealth at his disposal, to execute the long contemplated project," Hollingsworth, at the end of the novel, remains "depressed" and "melancholy" (242). Although he is drawn to Priscilla, she does not occupy his entire attention. As his "guardian" (242), she supports and sustains him, but Zenobia's "vindictive shadow dogged the side where Priscilla was not" (243). And Priscilla, although still "submissive" and "unquestioning," has her "happiness" "veiled" by Hollingsworth's "self-distrustful weakness" (242).

The "Arcadian freedom" that so disturbed Priscilla's and Hollingsworth's world influences Zenobia's sphere in an even more drastic way. Although she at first seems to be enchanted by Hollingsworth, she really shares his initial incapacity for love, albeit for different reasons. She is too self-centered to allow her attention to be caught and absorbed by a single object. She differs from both Priscilla and Hollingsworth in that she constantly changes both her inner and her outer landscapes: "I should think it a poor and meagre nature, that is capable of but one set of forms, and must convert all the past into a dream, merely because the present happens to be unlike it" (165). Both Hollingsworth and Priscilla have their attentions fixed, he by the idea that obsesses him, she by his image. In both cases consciousness is paralyzed by and absorbed by one object, and the rest of the world is ruled out. Zenobia implicitly rejects such a reduction of man's possibilities. As she sees things, it is a very "circumscribed mind" (164) that cannot find room for more than one set of ideas or objects or "live only in one mode of life" (166).

Her relation to the world, then, is not that of the obsessed idealist or lover who is enchanted or absorbed by one object or interest. "Alive with a passionate intensity" (102), she is motivated by desire rather than love.[6] In her quest to enrich her life as much as possible, she seeks to bring people and things toward her, to fascinate the world rather than to be fascinated by one part of it. She surrounds herself with "gorgeousness" which to Coverdale seems the "fulfillment of every fantasy of an imagination, revelling in various methods of costly self-indulgence and splendid ease" (164). Even while at Blithedale, she retains her "brilliant," "rare," and "costly" flower, and this flower more than the luxury of her city drawing room indicates that her relationship to

[6] "However, our desire does not lead toward the desired object but, on the contrary, our soul pulls away from the desired object toward itself. That is why it is very accurate to say that the object *awakens* a desire, as if to indicate that it does not participate in the process of desiring itself, but rather that its role ends when it stimulates desire, leaving us to do the rest. The psychological phenomenon of desire and that of 'being enchanted' produce reverse reactions. In the first, the object tends to be absorbed, while in the second the 'I' is absorbed. Appetite, therefore, does not result in surrender of oneself but, on the contrary, in the capture of the object" (Ortega, *On Love*, pp. 176–177).

the world is not grounded on self-surrender but on a desire
that pulls all things toward her.

   Here then is the context that best explains that Zenobia's
feeling for Hollingsworth does not take the form of Priscilla's "engrossing love" (220). Zenobia is not drawn hyp-
notically toward him but instead seeks to use her money and
her beauty to pull him toward herself. Her suicide, therefore, as Coverdale implies, is not an expression of the fact
that, as a lover, her well-being depends exclusively on the
beloved's generosity but rather is a willful response to the
feeling that "*everything* had failed her—prosperity, in the
world's sense, for her opulence was gone—the heart's prosperity, in love. And there was a secret burthen on her"
(239) [italics mine]. Priscilla, on the other hand, confronted by the threatening intimacy between Zenobia and
Hollingsworth, responds instinctively as if her substance or
reality were fading away. "Yet, at that instant, I saw her
droop. The buoyancy, which just before had been so bird-
like, was utterly departed; the life seemed to pass out of her,
and even the substance of her figure to grow thin and gray.
I almost imagined her a shadow, fading gradually into the
dimness of the wood" (125). In contrast to Priscilla's will-
less drifting toward death is the theatricality, the "tint of
Arcadian affection" (237) that characterizes Zenobia's
suicide, and the "terrible inflexibility" (235) of her lifeless
limbs suggests that in her case death is not so much the result of a loss of substance as it is a consequence of becoming
nothing but substance.

   Coverdale too finds it difficult, if not impossible, to fall in
love. He, like Zenobia, is incapable of the self-surrender love
demands, although he does not share her impulse to pull

everything within her own orbit. In his case, preoccupation with his own individuality prevents him from committing himself totally to another. As Zenobia scornfully tells him, his interest in the fates of his friends reveals a "monstrous skepticism in regard to any conscience or any wisdom, except one's own; a most irreverent propensity to thrust Providence aside, and substitute one's self in its awful place" (170). As the legend of the veiled lady makes clear, a commitment to this mode of perception precludes the possibility of one's ever being joined to another person. Coverdale, like Theodore in Zenobia's story, wishes others to be present for him without his being present for them, to be able visually to enter their spheres without the concomitant invasion of his own. He sees himself as a detached but sympathetic witness of the conduct of others, a "speculator on [their] motives" (163). Such a detached relationship with externality transforms the shared world of others from a reality capable of impinging on and transforming Coverdale's own sphere into an image that can be looked at and handed over to the imagination to interpret and to shape as it chooses. It is in this sense that Coverdale can turn the "whole affair into a ballad" (223).

Such an analysis, however, fails to account for Coverdale's final confession, the revelation by a man in his "afternoon" of life of a secret love of his youth. Because Coverdale is the narrator as well as a character in the narrative, the confession raises the question of intent as well as that of content and in that sense introduces issues similar to those found in Hawthorne's prefaces. There he seeks to by-pass the problem of intentionality in two ways: by introducing the figure of a fictive author and by insisting on the autonomy of the world of romance. The effect of these strategies, however, is to increase rather than to relieve the tension between fiction and reality. But *The Blithedale Romance* is a first-person narrative, a form distinguished by the fact that in it the realms of action (adventure) and writing are joined. The worlds of character and author, while not the same world, are nevertheless continuous ones. The middle-aged narrator is partially separated from his earlier youthful self but is not "altogether changed from the young man, who once hoped strenuously, and struggled, not so much amiss" (247).

The distance between past and present, unlike that between fiction and reality, can be reduced if not closed completely, through the process of recalling and articulating experiences from the past. Previously concealed patterns may surface, leading to a more profound understanding of the past than was possible at the time of action. For example, Coverdale emphasizes that his confession "brief as it shall be, will throw a gleam of light over my behavior throughout the foregoing incidents, and is, indeed, essential to the full understanding of my story" (247). The light of Coverdale's confession, however, is not immediately and unambiguously illuminating. To begin with, there is some evidence that his confession is not offered, as traditionally is the case, as an admission of guilt; on the contrary, it is presented by Coverdale in the form of an explanation and justification for his actions. Once the reader knows that the narrator has been in love with Priscilla, he can no longer accept at face value Zenobia's condemnation of the poet as a detached, cynical, and self-centered observer of other people's troubles. His interest in the affairs of his three acquaintances is now understood to be personal rather than purely aesthetic or voyeuristic. Coverdale, in other words, seeks to prove his innocence by employing a process usually reserved for the admission of guilt. The bad faith involved in such a procedure is obvious. As one student of the tradition of the confession has noted, "all confession, literary or sacramental, is either a lie or the record of a conversion, a death and a resurrection. Self-knowledge is necessarily death of the self, descent into Hell, while self-expression in its profoundest sense is necessarily a re-birth."[7] There is no sense of rebirth at the end of *The Blithedale Romance*, a novel that is, after all, the record of the failure of a search for a new life. Coverdale's life at the time of writing remains an alienated and fragmented one: he flings an "unsatisfied retrospect . . . back on life," describes the present as "all an emptiness," and casts a "bitter glance toward the future" (247).

But even if one sees Coverdale's confession as evidence that, as Roland Barthes asserts, the "retrospective is never anything but a category of bad faith,"[8] perhaps one can still value it as a form of self-reading that provides an important interpretive clue to the meaning of the narrative. As Coverdale says, the final pages of his history that constitute his confession are retained for his "individual and sole behoof" (245) and in this respect recall his earlier description of his tree-top hermitage, which, as his one exclusive possession at Blithedale, "symbolized [his] individuality and aided [him]

[7] John Freccero, "Zeno's Last Cigarette," *Modern Language Notes*, 77 (1962), p. 9.

[8] Roland Barthes, *Critical Essays*, trans. Richard Howard (Evanston, Ill.: Northwestern University Press, 1972), p. xi.

in keeping it inviolate" (99). And yet his words do not give
the reader an immediate and intimate access to Coverdale's
consciousness. Like the autobiographical elements of Hawthorne's prefaces, the personal material Coverdale offers
here is more mystifying than revealing. For one thing, the
concern with self it suggests is inconsistent with Hawthorne's understanding of love. As he sees it, love is a part
of one's secret life and cannot be talked about.[9] To confess
self-consciously to being in love as Coverdale does is to
admit that one is not enchanted and absorbed by another
person. Coverdale's confession, in short, like his hermitage,
is both an expression of the loneliness he suffers as a result
of his isolation from others and, at the same time, a recognition that any close relationship carries with it the threat that
one's own being will be merged with another's and one's
distinctiveness lost in the process. It is both "sad and dangerous . . . to be in too close affinity with the passions, the
errors, and the misfortunes, of individuals who stood within
a circle of their own" (205–206).

The act of writing down his story, then, is consistent
with the other acts in Coverdale's life. His relation to his
reader parallels his relation to other people in general. If the
reader accepts the confession at face value, then he must explain the fact that the prior relationship between himself
and the narrator has been grounded on a lie. The structure
of intersubjective relationships, which is the substance of
Coverdale's story, has been presented without an element
that would change its entire configuration. Nor is the introduction of the missing element the result of Coverdale's

[9] For this reason Hawthorne could not bring himself to inform
his mother and sisters of his engagement to Sophia (see Chapter 1).

attaining a deeper understanding of himself as he works his way through his past toward himself in the present. The act of writing his story is not for him, as it is for some first-person narrators, one that leads to an authentic vision of his life. The reverse is true. Coverdale does not write in an attempt to come to terms with his own life but to open an intercourse with the world on his own terms. The act of writing for him is another strategy for attaining the privileged position he needs in order to initiate relations with others. As a young man, he had sought to enter the presence of his Blithedale associates without in any way modifying the preexisting structure of relationships.

I felt an invincible reluctance, nevertheless, at the idea of presenting myself before my old associates, without first ascertaining the state in which they were. . . . Had it been evening, I would have stolen softly to some lighted window of the old farm-house, and peeped darkling in, to see all their well-known faces round the supper-board. Then, were there a vacant seat, I might noiselessly unclose the door, glide in, and take my place among them, without a word. My entrance might be so quiet, my aspect so familiar, that they would forget how long I had been away, and suffer me to melt into the scene, as a wreath of vapor melts into a larger cloud. [206–207]

Coverdale here seeks a privileged position from which to establish relations with others. Before approaching his old associates he seeks to "spy out" their "posture . . . as craftily as the wild Indian before he makes his onset" (207). He attempts to see them as a part of a lived experience from which he is as yet absent. In this way they can be viewed objectively, judged, and placed without the disturbing complications that would result if he were forced to consider the implications of his own place in their experience. The

ideal situation, of course, is the one of which he wistfully
dreams: a situation whereby he could exist *with* his associates while controlling the way he exists *for* them. As a
storyteller such a relationship seems available to him. As he
writes, he sits alone in his bachelor quarters with no fear of
direct involvement with others and self-consciously creates
the appearance he wishes to offer his readers at the same
time that he tells the story of his and his associates' experience at Blithedale. But the very fact that he writes for a
reader deprives his activity of the spontaneity of pure remembering, and its absence alerts the reader to the implications of Coverdale's indirection. As we have seen, his final
sentences do not successfully mediate between himself and
his reader. Instead they cause the reader to stand "in a position of new hostility, rather than new brotherhood" (20),
for they put into question the authenticity of a previously
established relationship.

But what of Hawthorne, the man who is playing the role
of an imaginary character who has obvious similarities to
himself and who is using events from his life as the basis for
the novel? There is little doubt that, as Arlin Turner has
said, Coverdale is the "most extensively autobiographical
character in Hawthorne's fiction."[10] Coverdale, however, is
also a veil or disguise Hawthorne wears and as such is both
a manifestation of Hawthorne and, at the same time, a dis-
tortion that alters that manifestation. Hawthorne, like
Coverdale, is a novelist interested in the secret lives of
others, but he is also a successful lover and husband. Indeed,
most of the happy lovers in his fiction are veiled versions of

[10] See his "Introduction" to the W. W. Norton edition of *The
Blithedale Romance* (New York, 1958), p. 23.

his relation to Sophia—a relation that appears to have been an extraordinarily happy one—and yet the fact that it is precisely the happiness of these lovers that distances them from the narrators who tell their stories implies that Hawthorne's communion with his wife, however perfect, can never be the model for his relations with others. Nevertheless that personal relationship exists beneath the surface of the fiction and serves to make a fundamental issue there, that of the relation between the hidden and the shown, the latent and the manifest. To discover the meaning of the fiction, therefore, is to discover a hidden content, the personal core concealed behind the substitutions and displacements that characterize the act of writing. This suggests that realms of lover and novelist—by extension the personal and social—may not be totally unrelated. It is true that the lover makes an open, spontaneous commitment to the beloved while the novelist seeks a veiled relationship with another; that the lover, enchanted by the dream of a "solitude of a united two," seeks seclusion while the novelist alone in his haunted chamber attempts to open an intercourse with the world. Still, the fact that the written text, like the veil of the lady in Zenobia's legend, holds open the possibility of a revelation at the same time that it conceals implies that the relation between writer and reader may lead to an intimacy similar to that enjoyed by lovers. For Hawthorne the fascination of reading like the fascination of love is the result of the irresistible lure exerted by another person's existence, but, unlike the relation between the beloved and the lover, that between author and reader is generated by a will to power.

4

The Enchantment of Reading

Fiction is to the grown man what play is to the child; it is there that he changes the atmosphere and tenor of his life; and when the game so chimes with his fancy that he can join in it with all his heart, when it pleases him with every turn, when he loves to recall it and dwells upon its recollection with entire delight, fiction is called romance.

> Robert Louis Stevenson,
> "A Gossip on Romance"

There are thus two interpretations of interpretation. . . . The one seeks to decipher, dreams of deciphering, a truth or an origin which is free from freeplay and from the order of the sign, and lives like an exile the necessity of interpretation. The other, which is no longer turned toward the origin, affirms freeplay and tries to pass beyond man and humanism.

> Jacques Derrida, "Structure, Sign, and Play
> in the Discourse of the Human Sciences"

For Hawthorne the act of reading is a compelling, mysterious, perhaps even dangerous occupation. Writers, after all, possess strange powers of enchantment that allow them to cast hypnotic spells over their readers as Holgrave does to Phoebe when he reads her his story of Alice Pyncheon. His words are like a "veil" that by enveloping her insures that she will "behold only him, and live only in his thoughts and emotions" (*CE* II, 211). Moreover, the writer does not actually have to be present to produce such a response. Septimius Felton experiences a similar effect as he reads an old manuscript whose unknown author is long since dead.

He caught the temper of the old writer's mind, after so many ages as that tract had lain in the mouldy and musty manuscript. He was magnetized with him; a powerful intellect acted powerfully upon him; perhaps, even, there was a sort of spell and mystic influence imbued into the paper, and mingled with the yellow ink, that steamed forth by the effort of this young man's earnest rubbing, as it were, and by the action of his mind, applied to it as intently as he possibly could; and even his handling the paper, his bending over it, and his breathing upon it, had its effect. [*CW* XI, 338]

Septimius is clearly enchanted by the act of reading, but it is not simply the text that fascinates him. It is the author who is present in the text as in " 'Arabian Nights' " a "demon" is present in a lamp or "copper vase" (388). And the relationship between the Aladdin-like reader and the mysterious demon is a curious and complicated one. Like Aladdin's lamp in the junk pile, a book on a shelf or table seems no more than one object among others with no special powers or attractions. And yet there lurks within the materials of its cover and pages a presence capable, it may be, of transforming the world. But that magical spirit can be released only if a reader, perhaps in search of other worlds, mysterious treasure, or, as in the case of Septimius, the formula for an elixir of youth, rubs its surface by the "action of his mind." Once the demon is released, however, he is the one in control. The price the reader pays for his curious desire is to be pulled away from the real world and delivered through the unreality of language into the mental universe of another. He is not only surrounded by strange words, images, and ideas, but he is in control of the alien principle who is their source.[1] In this sense the act of reading perfectly "illustrates the miraculous power of one human being over the will and passions of another" (*CE* III, 206). Hawthorne's fiction, of course, contains a number of dark enchanters who in their relations to their victims illustrate the effect of writers on readers. Westervelt—to mention one of a number of possible examples—who resembles "one of the enchanters of the Arabian Nights" (199), casts a veil over Priscilla which removes her to another world and makes her unconscious of being "the central object to all those straining eyes" (201).

[1] See Georges Poulet's description of the act of reading in "Criticism and the Experience of Interiority" in *The Languages of Criticism and the Sciences of Man*, eds. Richard Macksey and Eugenio Donato (Baltimore: The Johns Hopkins University Press, 1970), pp. 56–88.

Still, the situation of the reader differs in one important way from that of Priscilla. He does not require the intervention of some outside force to break the enchantment. The writer's spell over him is shattered when he turns the final page of the novel. Given this guarantee, there seems little reason why the reader should not freely submit himself to the author's wiles and fully enjoy the undeniable pleasures of immersing himself in a world that does not exist. Unfortunately, there is some evidence in Hawthorne's writings that he feels such a procedure would be cause for regret. The theme of mystification is a recurring one in his fiction and is usually related to those subversive caricatures of romance scattered throughout his writings. Familiar examples include Alymer's laboratory, Edward Hamilton's portrait of Edgar Vaughan, and Rappaccini's garden, but more useful ones for exploring the relation between enchantment and disenchantment are the sylvan dance and carnival episodes in *The Marble Faun*. Here Hawthorne examines the problem of the relation between self and others and explores the possibility that man's powers of enchantment may provide him with a way to mediate between them.

The grounds of the Villa Borghese, site of the sylvan dance, seem to imply that art can provide a release from the natural, historical, and social forces that imprison men and condemn them to a life of constant conflict. Here there is "enough of human care . . . bestowed long ago, and still bestowed, to prevent wildness from growing into deformity, and the result is an ideal landscape, a woodland scene, that seems to have been projected out of a poet's mind" (*CE* IV, 72). Here the "soft turf of a beautiful seclusion"

(70) offers welcomed relief from the "stony-hearted streets" (75) of Rome. Here the "ancient dust, the mouldiness of Rome . . . the hard pavements, the smell of ruin, and decaying generations; the chill palaces, the convent-bells, the heavy incense of altars . . . [rise] from . . . consciousness like a cloud" (74). Consequently, people of all social ranks and nationalities may meet and celebrate their shared freedom. Because each person seems equal to the rest, they all are able to participate in a "sylvan dance" which celebrates a new transparency and total reciprocity. "Here, as it seemed, had the Golden Age come back again, within the precincts of this sunny glade; thawing mankind out of their cold formalities; releasing them from irksome restraint; mingling them together in such childlike gaiety, that new flowers . . . sprang up beneath their footsteps" (88).

Unfortunately, however, such visions of harmony are the result of a mystification produced by the hallucinating air of a present freed from its ties to past and future. " 'Tomorrow will be time enough to come back to my reality.' " Miriam decides. " 'Is the past so indestructible? The future so immitigable?' " (82). And as she gives herself up to the "magic" (87) of the moment, reality seems transformed into fantasy. But this enchantment is no more than a delusion. The grounds of the "suburban Villa" do not duplicate the landscape of an unfallen world. Just the reverse is true: "Scattered here and there, with careless artifice, stand old altars, bearing Roman inscriptions. . . . But even these sportive imitations, wrought by man in emulation of what Time has done to temples and palaces, are perhaps centuries old, and, beginning as illusions, have grown to be venerable in sober earnest" (72–73). As a result of this artifice, the grounds are "pensive, lovely, dreamlike, enjoyable, and sad" (73). And adding to the "dreamlike melancholy that haunts the spot" (73), is malaria, a curse that insures it will never be the "home-scenery of any human being" (73), for it can be safely visited only in winter and early spring.

Initially, then, the grounds were the product of a vision that sought to mediate between man and nature through the employment of a mild irony. They were designed not as a Quixotic attempt to assert an identification between the two but in an attempt to come to terms with a basic difference by reflecting on it. The result is the creation of a place where man seeks partially to alleviate his alienation by indulging in a gentle nostalgia for an imagined time of a lost unity. Man's "sportive" imitations of the effects of time seem to place him outside those effects and to protect him from them. This possibility, however, is put into question by the narrator's description of the final moments of the sylvan dance.

Or it [the dance] was like the sculptured scene on the front and sides of a sarcophagus, where, as often as any other device, a festive procession mocks the ashes and white bones that are treasured up, within. You might take it for a marriage-pageant; but, after a while, if you look attentively at these merry-makers, following them from end to end of the marble coffin, you doubt whether their gay movement is leading them to a happy close. . . . Always, some tragic incident is shadowed forth, or thrust sidelong into the spectacle; and when once it has caught your eye, you can look no more at the festal portions of the scene, except with reference to this one slightly suggested doom and sorrow. [88]

Here art is clearly relegated to the status of a mystified defensive strategy which seeks to avoid the temporal predica-

ment that renders man's life meaningless. Like the succession
of discontinuous movements of the sylvan dance—"each
vanished with the moment that gave it birth, and was
effaced from memory by another" (85)—the figures on the
sarcophagus seem to imply the supremacy of art over nature
through the transcendence of the effects of temporal dura-
tion. The "unweariable steps" (88) of the dancers mock
the "demon of Weariness" (336) who haunts the streets of
Rome in the same way that the figures on the sarcophagus
mock the "ashes and white bones" it contains. At the very
moment man is celebrating his powers of renewal, however,
the destructive powers of time are secretly at work. The
dance is moving toward its conclusion as inevitably as the
figures in the marriage-pageant are toward the "ashes and
white bones" they at first seem to transcend. From the point
of view of death all human activity has the "character of
fantasy." "The spell being broken, it was now only that old
tract of pleasure-ground, close by the people's gate of
Rome; a tract where crimes and calamities of ages, the
many battles, blood recklessly poured out, and deaths of
myriads, have corrupted all the soil, creating an influence
that makes the air deadly to human lungs" (90).

The "suburban gardens," then, can offer no real escape
from the threatening atmosphere of Rome. The "enchanted
ground" (75) at best can provide no more than a moment's
mystification, and the disenchantment that inevitably follows invalidates the mildly ironic vision that produced the
grounds in the first place. The pleasant nostalgia for a lost
relationship between man and nature that the grounds are
intended to evoke is replaced at the moment of disenchantment with a painful intersubjective problem.

A moment afterwards [the appearance of Miriam's model] Donatello was aware that she had retired from the dance. He hastened towards her and flung himself on the grass, beside the stone-bench on which Miriam was sitting. But a strange distance and unapproachableness had all at once enveloped her; and though he saw her within reach of his arm, yet the light of her eyes seemed as far off as that of a star; nor was there any warmth in the melancholy smile with which she regarded him. [89]

Donatello and Miriam have not been able to use the gardens to bridge the "great chasm" (207) that separates them. He, it is true, is the representation of a condition that once existed between man and nature and seems able to identify himself with the non-self, but neither that sense of identification nor man's self-conscious remembering of it can ever mediate between him and another self.

But if human separateness cannot be overcome by a self-conscious return to nature through art perhaps man can direct his powers of enchantment toward his own constructs, the forms and usages of civilization, and force those laws of restraint to mediate between isolated selves. Miriam and Donatello explore this possibility when they participate in the "scenic and ceremonial" (436) carnival, near the end of the novel. Having failed in their earlier attempts to transform themselves into Faun and Nymph, they adorn themselves with masks and costumes and become "The Peasant and the Contadina" (439). In the carnival there is a "sympathy of nonsense; a true and genial brotherhood and sisterhood, based on the honest purpose . . . of being foolish, all together" (439). Perhaps the "sympathetic mirth" (438) of others, the "sympathetic exhilaration of so many people's cheerfulness" (324) will enable them to bridge the

distance between them. In contrast to the magic of the
sylvan dance, which thaws the participants out of their cold
formalities and mingles them together in a "childlike gaiety"
(88), the spell of the carnival seeks to unite men by recog-
nizing and exaggerating the distance that separates them
from nature and each other. Here one finds "orang-outanges;
bear-headed, bull-headed, and dog-headed individuals; faces
that would have been human, but for their enormous
noses . . . and all other imaginable kind of monstrosity
and exaggeration" (446). These disguises hardly represent
nostalgic attempts to recover some lost resemblance between man and nature. Rather they imply a comic recognition of the differences between the two realms and are an
implicit affirmation of the superiority of the human. Men
are brought closer together when any assertion of a resemblance between the human and natural is made to seem un-
tenable. In a similar way the other costumes and masks,
which from the point of view of unclothed nature imply
human separateness and civilized restraint, in the context of
the carnival suggest relief from the burdens of class and
profession and protection from the dangers of the threatening gaze of others, for they allow individuals to form a
"mad, merry stream of human life" (439).

The carnival, too, however, is the product of a deceitful
magic that covers a "stern and black reality" with "fanciful
thoughts" (428), and the "sympathetic mirth" (438) it
generates, is "like our self-deceptive pretense of jollity at a
threadbare joke" (437). Hence, the sugarplums the participants throw at one another "were concocted mostly of
lime, with a grain or oats or some other worthless kernel in
the midst" (439), and the carnival of flowers, which have

been "gathered and tied up by sordid hands," are "wilted," "muddy," and "defiled . . . with the wicked filth of Rome" (440). The carnival, in short, is the "emptiest of mockeries" (437), composed of a host of absurd figures who in "pretending to sympathize" (446) with one another only make more obvious the absence of any real sympathy. Miriam, a participant in the "sad frolic" (446) hides a "tear-stained face" beneath her mask and speaks with a "profound sadness in her tone" (448). Appropriately, she and Donatello are arrested by the authorities at the height of the revelry, and their arrest is misinterpreted as "some frolic of the Carnival, carried a little too far" (451).

In the sylvan dance and carnival episodes Hawthorne dramatizes the basic problem of romance, which arises from man's attempt to use his powers of enchantment to solve an important intersubjective conflict through the creation of a "neutral territory." At first he seems successful, but that impression is then shown to be the result of the mystifying effect of the enchantment. Even worse, one does not return untouched from enchanted realms. Many of Hawthorne's characters, like Alonzo Quijano at the end of *Don Quixote*, are driven toward melancholy or death by their moments of enchantment. For Miriam and Donatello the enchantments initiate a destructive process leading to murder in the first case and to their arrest in the second. Hester Prynne, after being enchanted by her idyllic forest meeting with Dimmesdale, not only loses the hopes engendered by that magical encounter but comes to experience that moment when they were lovers as an inaccessible anteriority. "She thought of the dim forest, with its little dell of solitude, and love, and anguish. . . . How deeply had they known each other

then! And was this the man? She hardly knew him
now . . . ! Her spirit sank with the idea that all must have
been a delusion, and that, vividly as she had dreamed it,
there could be no real bond betwixt the clergyman and herself" (*CE* I, 239–240). Finally, Sylph Etherege, having been
"wiled . . . away to shadow-land" (*CW* III, 516) by
Edward Hamilton's creation of her "phantom lover," dies
as soon as her "dream is rudely broken," and she is brought
back to the "truths and realities of life" (515).

The experiences of these disillusioned victims of enchantment, obviously, are disturbing to readers of romance, for
their experiences put into question the possibility of any
innocent form of enchantment. Hawthorne's reader, however, does not approach the fictive world innocently or
naively. He is introduced to that world by a preface in a
way that insures he will not be enchanted as Hester and
Sylph are. Hawthorne's prefaces function to demystify the
writer-reader relationship by revealing the disturbing and
complex motives behind the acts of writing and reading.
To begin with, the prefaces confirm that Hawthorne's decision to become a writer is not one he arrives at easily and
unquestioningly. The decision to become a "fiction-monger"
(*CW* III, 387), to spend his life in a "haunted chamber"
(*LL* I, 223) recording with "benumbed fingers" his imaginings of "passions," "feelings," "of all states of the heart
and mind" (225), is more problematical for him than for
most writers. Since writing is not a viable profession for an
American in the 1830's, especially for one whose youthful
productions show little promise and who receives little encouragement to continue writing, a "reasonable prospect of
reputation or profit" does not exist. There is nothing but

the "pleasure itself of composition—an enjoyment not at all amiss in its way . . . but which, in the long run, will hardly keep the chill out of a writer's heart, or the numbness out of his fingers" (*CE* IX, 3). Only the knowledge that he is being "read," that the public is not treating him with a "total lack of sympathy" (3) can begin to justify his decision to become a writer, for his commitment to writing, finally, is the result of his attempt to solve the problem of his solitude. His tales, he believes, are not the "written communications of a solitary mind with itself," but rather attempts "to open an intercourse with the world" (6).

Such communication, however, is indirect at best. Writing, after all, is a solitary act, carried out behind the "bolts and bars" of a "lonely chamber" (*LL* I, 224), and its immediate effect is to immerse the author in a world that does not exist, rather than to put him in touch with other people. Nevertheless the finished book is intended for the eyes of others. Sooner or later the writer's visions may "become visible to the world" (223). Still, he does not actively reach out toward the world of others. Having committed his words to paper he sits and waits for the world to acknowledge his existence: "and here I sat a long, long time, waiting patiently for the world to know me, and sometimes wondering why it did not know me sooner, or whether it would ever know me at all—at least, till I were in my grave. . . . By and bye, the world found me out in my lonely chamber, and called me forth" (*LL* I, 223–224).

By introducing himself indirectly to others through his writing Hawthorne seems able to achieve a unique and privileged position. He sits passively and safely in the protective darkness of his writing chamber and awaits recogni-

tion from others. He manages, in short, through his fiction
to exist for others without first offering himself to their
judgment. His readers first "conceive the sort of kindness
for the book which a person naturally feels for a discovery
of his own" and then "extend" that "kindly feeling" to the
"Author" (*CE* IX, 7). This flow of sentiment, moreover,
moves only in one direction and is the result of an act of
interpretation rather than a direct human encounter, for the
author's words do not represent him in his own proper
character. The "mild, shy, gentle, melancholic, exceedingly
sensitive, and not very forcible man" whom the reader accepts as author is no real person at all but simply an image
the reader has constructed from "internal evidence of [the]
sketches." This interpreted self is then accepted by the
author to the extent that his "subsequent productions" are
"influenced and modified by a natural desire to fill up so
amicable an outline, and to act in consonance with the character assigned to him." In such a way the imprisoning walls
of the haunted chamber are removed: "these volumes have
opened the way to the most agreeable associations, and to
the formations of imperishable friendships" (7).

The act of writing, then, seems to allow Hawthorne to
maintain a distinction between his own inwardness and his
social being, to cultivate the appearance of "confidential
intimacy" (*CW* III, 385) and still keep the "inmost Me
behind its veil" (*CE* I, 4). Because no important "disclosure" is made (*CW* III, 385), public and private existence
have no common denominator, with the result that Hawthorne seems able to protect himself from the dangers of
involvement and participate in the benefits that derive from
a shared life with others. By freely offering the public an

invented self, he is able to modify the structure of human relationships, because he does not stand in the place where others expect to find him. The character of the speaker in the prefaces exists—to use Sartre's precise phrasing—on the plane of the for-others, and so long as the reader identifies the author with that character the real Hawthorne escapes him.[2]

This remarkable strategy, of course, depends for its success on the acceptance by author and reader of the conventional view of their relationship. Hawthorne seeks to guarantee that acceptance by introducing "each of his humble publications with a familiar kind of Preface" (*CE* IV, 1). By using such an "antique fashion of Preface" (1), he hopes to be granted a "certain conventional privilege" which in the "old countries" is "awarded to the romancer" (*CE* III, 1–2). Although the human situation is such that it is "scarcely decorous . . . to speak at all, even when we speak impersonally" (*CE* I, 4), within the context of the convention of the familiar preface an "author . . . may be autobiographical without violating the reader's rights or his own" (4). Both writer and reader assume traditional roles and let those roles mediate their relationship. When a "prim

[2] Sartre, discussing the character of Proust's hero writes: "so long as the reader using the usual optic process of reading identifies himself with the hero of the novel, the character of 'Marcel' escapes him: better yet it does not exist on this level. It appears only if I break the complicity which unites me to the writer, only if I consider the book no longer as a confidant but as a confidence, still better as a document. This character exists therefore only on the plane of the for-others, and that is the reason why the teachings and descriptions of 'psychological realists' . . . are never discovered in the lived experience of the subject" (*Being and Nothingness,* p. 325).

old author" addresses himself to an "Honored Reader" who
is "Kind," "Gentle," and "Indulgent," the rules of decorum
governing that relationship will prevent it, he hopes, from
becoming aggressively personal.

Nevertheless, Hawthorne's strategy is not without its
dangers. His public identity, after all, is based entirely on
the interpretation of others and depends completely on their
generosity. When the readers decide not to accept the
traditional role the author assigns them and respond to his
writings in a personal and unsympathetic way, a number of
complications appear that require modifications in the
writer's initial strategy.

Some of the more crabbed of my critics, I understand, have
pronounced your friend egotistical, indiscreet, and even im-
pertinent, on account of the Prefaces and Introductions with
which, on several occasions, he has seen fit to pave the reader's
way into the interior edifice of a book. . . .

But the charge, I am bold to say, is not a reasonable one, in
any view which we can fairly take of it. There is no harm,
but, on the contrary, good, in arraying some of the ordinary
facts of life in a slightly idealized and artistic guise. I have taken
facts which relate to myself, because they chance to be nearest
at hand, and likewise are my own property. And, as for ego-
tism, a person, who has been burrowing, to his utmost ability,
into the depths of our common nature, for the purposes of
psychological romance . . . will smile at incurring such an
imputation in virtue of a little preliminary talk about his external habits, his abode, his casual associates, and other matters entirely upon the surface. These things hide the man, instead of
displaying him. You must make quite another kind of inquest,
and look through the whole range of his fictitious characters,
good and evil, in order to detect any of his essential traits.   [*CW*
III, 385–386]

Apparently a secret knowledge that others cannot truly know him is not enough to put Hawthorne at ease. He seems troubled by his reader's failure to recognize and accept the rules of the convention he employs. To be misunderstood, it seems, is as threatening as to be completely transparent, for in both cases one is captured by the judging eye of the other. His freedom depends upon his ability to remain enigmatic to others. Therefore he deliberately violates his chosen convention by exposing the fictive nature of the seemingly authoritative voice of his prefaces, hoping that such a strategy will disconcert his audience. This voice, he implies, is as much a fictional invention as the stories or novel it introduces. It cannot be taken as the true voice of Nathaniel Hawthorne. Just the reverse is true. It is a protective mask hiding the real author from the reader's probing eye. And once the true function of the convention is laid bare, the reader is again on the defensive.

Nevertheless, Hawthorne does hold open the possibility that his "essential traits" may still be found if only after a complete reading and careful interpretation of all his writings. Quite clearly, what he seeks in the prefaces is both to attract and confuse his reader. On the one hand, his insistence that his fictional use of personal details hides rather than reveals his true nature insures him a privileged position while, on the other, his hint that the proper inquest will unveil the "inmost Me" tempts the reader by holding open the possibility of a truly intimate relationship. His veil at once conceals and entices the reader to imagine the features behind it.

The result of this focus on prying and concealing is to discredit the writer's motives and to make it impossible for the reader to enjoy an innocent relation to his text. Indeed, the emphasis in the prefaces on the relation between the hidden and the revealed in his work creates a suspicious, probing reader who will carry out in reverse the author's work of falsification. The writer's guile will be met with a double guile of his own. Fascination will be countered by its opposite, interpretation—a tactic of suspicion designed to allow the reader to penetrate the writer's mask and demystify his illusions.[3] Like Septimius Felton, the reader will resist the author's attempt to enchant him by seeking to "decipher and interprete" (*CW* XI, 336) the hidden meaning of the text which seems to be "lock[ed] up for safety in a sort of coffer, of which diligence and insight should be the key, and the keen intelligence with which the meaning was sought should be the test of the seeker's being entitled to possess the secret treasure" (337). Here, as in his discussion of the form of his presence in his work, Hawthorne seems to suggest a relation in his fiction between the essential and inessential, whereby the essential will stand revealed when the superficial elements concealing it are in some way removed. He may be hidden in his text in the same way that for a sculptor "a figure is embedded in the stone, and must be freed from its encumbering superfluities" (*CW* IV, 115), or in the same way that the deeper meaning of Septimius' manuscript is hidden beneath the superficial surface of a "digested synopsis of some old philosopher's wise rules of conduct" (*CW* XI, 337). The essential, in

---

[3] I am indebted here to Paul Ricoeur's discussion of the problem of interpretation in *Freud and Philosophy*, trans. Denis Savage (New Haven: Yale University Press, 1970), pp. 3–56.

other words, may be grasped only after the inessential surface has been violated if not destroyed.

Obviously, the reader who is to relate to the text in this violent manner has little in common with that "Indulgent," "Gentle" reader so often invoked by Hawthorne. As a matter of fact, Hawthorne's conception of romance might be said to develop from a tension formed, on the one hand, by his dreams of a "Gentle Reader," who in his innocence and simplicity will accept at face value and be enchanted by the beautiful web woven by the romancer, and on the other by a knowledge that such a dream represents an impossible ideal since understanding and appreciation depend upon deciphering and interpreting, and those acts are necessarily violent ones.

The Gentle Reader, we trust, would not thank us for one of those minute elucidations, which are so tedious, and, after all, so unsatisfactory, in clearing up the romantic mysteries of a story. He is too wise to insist upon looking closely at the wrong side of the tapestry, after the right one has been sufficiently displayed to him, woven with the best of the artist's skill, and cunningly arranged with a view to the harmonious exhibition of its colours. If any brilliant or beautiful, or even tolerable, effect have been produced, this pattern of kindly Readers will accept it at its worth, without tearing the web apart, with the idle purpose of discovering how its threads have been knit together; for the sagacity, by which he is distinguished, will long ago have taught him that any narrative of human action and adventure—whether we call it history or romance—is certain to be fragile handiwork, more easily rent than mended. [*CE* IV, 455]

To seek the meaning of his tapestry, Hawthorne implies here, is to violate it in some way, to tear it, perhaps change

it. And yet an eye that never penetrates the surface of a
text is bound to miss that "indefinable nothing, that in-
estimable something, that constitutes [its] life and soul"
(*CE* IV, 60). It is this "inner mystery of a work of genius"
(391) that is the source of both its beauty and value. Moreover, the beautiful effect the writer seeks to produce invites
the very violence he deplores, for it is that "gleam of
beauty" that "induces[s] the beholder to start unravelling
it" (306).

The Gentle Reader invoked here does not exist. He belongs to a lost world of sympathetic involvement, a world
where understanding imposed no burden and an innocent
interpretation was possible. One of Hawthorne's models for
his imaginings of that lost happiness is natural man, a "beautiful creature, standing betwixt man and animal, sympathizing with each, comprehending the speech of either race,
and interpreting the whole existence of one to the other"
(*CE* IV, 13). Speaking in the "original voice and utterance
of the natural man" (248), which has since been "laid aside
and forgotten by other men, now that words have been
feebly substituted in the place of signs and symbols" (77–
78) this creature is free of the burden of interpretation.
"Before the sophistication of the human intellect formed
what we now call language" (249), the world interpreted
itself "without the aid of words" (258). In the place of
language that seeks through endless analogies to mediate the
distance now existing between man and nature, there once
was a power of sympathy that brought all parts of existence
together and allowed them to communicate instantly and
completely: "he was believed to possess gifts by which he
could associate himself with the wild things of the forests,

and with the fowls of the air, and could feel a sympathy even with the trees, among which it was his joy to dwell" (235).

But as Donatello's adventure in *The Marble Faun* makes clear, that state of sympathy that once may have united man to his milieu no longer exists. The young primitive loses that "power of sympathy" (320) that binds him to the natural world, and he finds it impossible to live the life of his forefathers. "He could not live their healthy life of animal spirits, in sympathy with Nature, and brotherhood with all that breathed around them. Nature, in beast, fowl, and tree, and earth, flood, and sky, is what it was of old; but sin, care, and self-consciousness have set the human portion of the world askew; and thus the simplest character is ever the surest to go astray" (239–240). Nor is it possible to discover the source or origin of that lost unity: "It would have been as difficult . . . to follow up the stream of Donatello's ancestry to its dim source, as travellers have found it, to reach the mysterious fountains of the Nile" (231).

The unbridgeable distance between the present moment and that lost moment of beginning is implied, too, by the fact that Donatello seems to his companions to resemble not a faun, but the representation of one, and that representation, moreover, is the expression of rather than the solution to a mystery. "Praxiteles has subtlely diffused, throughout his work, that mute mystery which so hopelessly perplexes us, whenever we attempt to gain an intellectual or sympathetic knowledge of the lower forms of creation" (10). The meaning of the statue, in short, is in the form of a "riddle," an unanswered question that is the sign of a primeval origin lost forever and available now only in the form of a "poet's reminiscence of a period when man's affinity with Nature was more strict, and his fellowship with every living thing more intimate and dear" (11).

Donatello's Arcadian unselfconsciousness, however, is not the only form of innocence Hawthorne imagines. Hilda's initial innocence does not manifest itself in the form of an enjoyment of the "warm, sensuous, earthly side of Nature" (13). As a "daughter of the puritans" (54), she is perplexed by Donatello's apparent affinity with nature. Her innocence is the result of a special relationship with divinity, for she looks at "humanity with angel's eyes" (55). She is a "poor, lonely girl, whom God has set here in an evil world, and given her only a white robe, and bid her wear it back to Him, as white as when she put it on" (208). Her innocence, therefore, takes the form of a "silent sympathy," not with nature but with the paintings of the Old Masters, those products that are at once the expression of man's highest accomplishments and the "true symbol of the glories of the better world, where a celestial radiance will be inherent in all things and persons, and render each continually transparent to the sight of all" (304). Like Spenser's land of Faery, the paintings mediate between mankind and a supernatural reality, and Hilda, by the use of a "guiding light of sympathy . . . went straight to the central point, in which the Master had conceived his work. Thus, she viewed it, as it were, with his own eyes, and hence her comprehension of every picture was perfect" (57).

For Hilda, as for Donatello, interpretation at first poses no problem. Other copyists work "entirely from the out-

side" and seek "only to reproduce the surface" (60), thereby representing the painting's superficial design but missing
the inner core of meaning, while Hilda, on the other hand,
is able to "interpret what the feeling is, that gives [the]
picture such a mysterious force" (65). Her interpretive
powers, of course, derive from her special relationship to
God—"I had only God to take care of me, and be my
closest friend" (359)—a relationship that validates the
religious themes of the "mighty Italian Masters" (336). The
crime she witnesses, however, destroys this relationship:
"the terrible, terrible crime, which I have revealed to you,
thrust itself between Him and me; so that I groped for Him
in the darkness, as it were, and found Him not—found
nothing but a dreadful solitude, and this crime in the midst
of it" (359). With the loss of her special relationship to
God comes a "dimness of insight," a loss of her powers of
"self-surrender . . . and sympathy" (335). In the place of
that lost sympathy, moreover, is substituted a "keen intellectual perception" that produces "irreverent" rather than
sympathetic criticism. "Heretofore, her sympathy went
deeply into a picture, yet seemed to leave a depth which it
was inadequate to sound; now, on the contrary, her perceptive faculty penetrated the canvas like a steel probe, and
found but a crust of paint over an emptiness" (341).

Hilda's knowledge of Miriam's and Donatello's crime,
then, makes an innocent interpretation impossible for her.
The process of understanding a painting is now one that
necessarily does violence to it. Even worse. The interpretive
act, which destroys the surface, does not reveal a core of
hidden meaning but instead uncovers an absence that im-

plies that the "pictorial art" may be "altogether a delusion" (336); and Hilda's earlier innocent response to it, therefore, is the result of a mystification.

The death of the Gentle Reader, which Hawthorne acknowledges in the preface to *The Marble Faun*, is really assumed in all of his prefaces, and his absence is the equivalent for the author of those losses experienced by Hilda and Donatello. Because the "Gentle Reader" lies beneath some "mossy grave-stone, inscribed with some half-obliterated name," the writer, deprived of "apprehensive sympathy," and surrounded by "unkindly eyes" which may "skim over what was never meant for them" is forced to "stand upon ceremony, now, and, after stating a few particulars about the work which is here offered to the Public . . . make [his] most reverential bow, and retire behind the curtain" (*CE* IV, 2). Like the ruins of Rome, the moss-covered stone that marks the grave of the Gentle Reader is not a memorial perpetuating a memory but the indicator of a lost significance. The "half-obliterated name" inscribed on it can never be recognized and the monument's meaning, therefore, consists of the absence of the memory it was designed to perpetuate.[4] And that sense of loss or absence determines the form of the writer's presence in his work, for it leads to his curtaining himself off from his reader. That moss-covered stone, however, is as much a sign of a yearning for "apprehensive sympathy" as it is a monument to continual loss. The very fact that he writes implies that the author hopes he will not remain completely hidden behind

---

[4] I am indebted here to Jean Starobinski's discussion of ruins in *The Invention of Liberty 1700–1789*, trans. Bernard C. Swift (Geneva: Skira, 1964), p. 180.

the curtain but will find some means of relating to a hostile reader. Indeed, most of the prefaces may be seen as attempts on the author's part to minimize or perhaps divert the interpretive violence that must necessarily follow a reader's encounter with a text. He seeks to "pave the reader's way into the interior edifice of a book" (*CW* III, 385), to protect the texture of his narrative from the "inflexible and exceedingly dangerous species of criticism" (*CE* II, 3) that seeks the meaning of a romance by comparing the fictive events with "actual events of real lives" (*CE* III, 1).

Or, to put the problem in another way, the prefaces explicitly deny the old view of the writer as a privileged creator who weaves an original web for an innocent reader, whose response to it is one of an unreflective beholding. It turns out that the writer as well as the reader must bear the burden of interpretation, for the act of creation is one of unweaving and reweaving the texts of others. Hawthorne's tales are "twice told" not only in the sense of being "musty and mouse-nibbled leaves of old periodicals, transformed by the magic arts of . . . friendly publishers into a new book" (*CW* III, 389), but also in the sense of being interpretations of events, objects, and stories from the past. His starting point as a writer is most often an "Old Time Legend," some object or scrap of gossip from the past pregnant with an undisclosed meaning he sets out to uncover or translate for his reader. The most explicit treatment of this theme, of course, is found in Hawthorne's discussion of the source of *The Scarlet Letter*. The story, he tells us, derives from his reading of a faded Scarlet A which presents itself as "most worthy of interpretation" (*CE* I, 32) and "several foolscap sheets, containing many particulars respecting the life and conversation of one Hester Prynne" (32). In both cases Hawthorne's reading is the last of a series of interpretations. As Charles Feidelson notes in his seminal discussion of this episode, everyone in the novel reenacts the scene in which Hawthorne attempts to read the meaning of the letter,[5] and the letter is interpreted in a variety of ways by Hester and her contemporaries as well as by Hawthorne and the reader. Hester herself, moreover, is the "text of the discourse[s]" (85) not only of puritan clergymen but also of the "aged persons, alive in the time of Mr. Surveyor Pue . . . from whose oral testimony he had made up his narrative," and his narrative, in turn, forms the basis of *The Scarlet Letter.* Hawthorne seeks to uncover then the "dark meaning" (31) in the faded A as well as the "traces of Mr. Pue's mental part, and the internal operations of his head" (30) contained in the "half a dozen sheets of foolscap" (33). And as Hawthorne is Pue's commentator so the reader is his, seeking in Hawthorne's text the elusive meaning of the mysterious A as well as the features of its current interpreter. No matter how interpretations proliferate, however, something will always remain hidden, for the wonderful A "gives evidence of a now forgotten art, not to be rediscovered even by the process of picking out the threads" (31).

The perspective suggested by the prefaces' relation to the texts that they introduce seems to provide a solution to the problem of Hawthorne's solitude at the same time it insures that that solution will not be at the expense of the reader. First, it acknowledges the inevitability of the self-other con-

[5] Charles Feidelson, *Symbolism and American Literature* (Chicago: University of Chicago Press, 1953), p. 10.

flict by associating the experience of mutuality with a moment of lost plentitude when men were mutually transparent and innocent interpretations possible. Next, it identifies any attempt to use the powers of the imagination to recover that lost moment as a subversive and threatening mystification capable of leading to melancholy and death. Finally, it offers as an alternative both to face-to-face encounters and mystified forms of mediation a mode of communication that maintains a tension between the hidden and the shown, thereby insuring that neither reader nor writer can ever be completely caught by the other. The writer's features can never be totally hidden behind the characters he assumes, but because those features exist in the form of a content that is not explicitly signified, the reader can never be certain that his investigation has revealed a complete picture. Consequently, romance, like the Scarlet A, has the privilege of showing while concealing, thereby insuring that something will always be left in reserve, undiscovered and unspoken, making it possible for the writer to speak to a potentially hostile audience about matters of which silence is the safest form of expression, and for the reader to respond to his words without the fear of becoming his mystified victim.[6]

[6] See Michel Foucault's discussion of commentary as an activity that tries to "transmit an old, unyielding discourse seemingly silent to itself, into another, more prolix discourse . . . to comment is to admit by definition an excess of signified over the signifier; a necessary, unformulated remainder of thought that language has left in the shade—a remainder that is the very essence of that thought, driven outside its secret—but to comment also presupposes that this unspoken element slumbers within speech (*parole*), and that, by a superabundance proper to the signifier, one may, in questioning it,

Romance, however, as fiction, has an ontological as well as an intersubjective dimension. The prefaces focus persistently on the problem of source or origin, and that focus reminds us that at both its beginnings and its endings fiction invites comparison with reality and is thereby revealed to be an illusion.[7] That revelation, of course, has important consequences for both writer and reader. As Hawthorne understands them, literary conventions have traditionally functioned as an attempt to by-pass this disenchanting encounter. In the same way that the Old World writers use the "Antique fashion of Preface" to mediate between hostile consciousnesses, they employ the convention of a "Faery Land" (*CE* III, 3), "a sort of poetic or fairy precinct" (*CE* IV, 3), a "neutral territory . . . where the Actual and Imaginary may meet, and each imbue itself with the nature of the other" (*CE* I, 36), in order to bridge the gap between fiction and reality. In the Old World such conventions can function successfully because there man remains committed to a hierarchical, essentialist metaphysic that allows him to resolve the difference between reality and representations of it. Spenser's *Fairy Queen*, for example, mediates between a fallen world and a distant God by revealing the analogues whereby natural objects are joined to a supernatural reality. For Hawthorne, however, as for

---

give voice to a content that was not explicitly signified" (*The Birth of the Clinic*, trans. A. M. Sheridan Smith [New York: Pantheon, 1973], p. xvi).

[7] See Edward W. Said's perceptive discussion of this problem in "Molestation and Authority in Narrative Fiction," in *Aspects of Narrative: Selected Papers from the English Institute*, ed. J. Hillis Miller (New York: Columbia University Press, 1971), pp. 47–68.

Cervantes, a conflict exists between the "gleaming waters and shadowy foliage" of man's dreams and desires and the "desert" (*CE* IV, 237) dryness of actuality, and this conflict implies a victory of one over the other, with the result that man seems destined to live either a hallucinated or disillusioned existence.[8]

In Hawthorne's world as in Keats' one alternates between a world of dreams and the cold hillside of reality. "What could the little bird mean by pouring it [a song] forth at midnight? Probably the note gushed out from the midst of a dream, in which he fancied himself in Paradise with his mate; and suddenly awakening, he found himself on a cold, leafless bough, with a New-England mist penetrating through his feathers. That was a sad exchange of imagination for reality" (*CE* VIII, 386). Such exchanges form the basic structure of Hawthorne's world: perpetual aspiration alternates with perpetual frustration.[9] Owen Warland's aspiring intentions are materialized, for he cannot "content himself with the inward enjoyment of the Beautiful, but must chase the flitting mystery beyond the verge of his ethereal domain, and crush its frail beauty in seizing it with a material grasp" (*CE* X, 458).

[8] Ortega argues that this conflict is basic to the novel's form. See his *Meditations on Quixote*, pp. 143–145.

[9] This is a characteristic Hawthorne shares with a number of other romantic writers. Geoffrey Hartman writes that "Romanticism at its most profound reveals the depth of the enchantments in which we live. We dream, we wake on the cold hillside, and our sole self pursues the dream once more. In the beginning was the dream, and the task of disenchantment never ends" ("Romanticism and Anti-Self Consciousness," *Beyond Formalism* [New Haven: Yale University Press, 1970], pp. 307–308).

A sensible man had better not let himself be betrayed into these attempts to realize the things which he has dreamed about, and which, when they cease to be purely ideal in his mind, will have lost the truest of their truth, the loftiest and profoundest part of their power over his sympathies. Facts, as we really find them, whatever poetry they may involve, are covered with a stony excrescence of prose, resembling the crust on a beautiful sea-shell, and they never show their most delicate and divinest colors, until we shall have dissolved away their grosser actualities by steeping them long in a powerful menstruum of thought. And, seeking to actualise them again, we do but renew the crust.   [*CE* V, 135–136]

Dreams and reality are unable to coexist as one always seeks to invade and transform the other's realm. The mind seeks to "relieve itself . . . from the cruel weight and hardness of the reality" (*CE* I, 51) by "spiritualizing the grossness of this actual life" (*CE* X, 185), while reality, on the other hand, solidifies or materializes the aspiring intentions by "thrusting itself through life's brightest illusions" (*CE* IV, 303).

Hawthorne's interest in a "neutral territory," an "intermediate space, where the business of life does not intrude" (*CW* I, 344) quite clearly derives in part from a desire to resolve the conflict between fiction and reality. And at times he seems to have been successful. In *The Scarlet Letter* and *The House of the Seven Gables* it is difficult to distinguish between fiction and history, imagination and perception. Nevertheless Hawthorne remains painfully aware of the fact that these balanced relationships exist only within the realm of the fictive, not in actuality. Hence his prefaces, which seem at first to assert the priority of fiction over reality, are pervaded by a sense of nostalgia, a longing of the heart for some other kind of fulfillment. A task has been completed, but it is followed by restlessness rather than tranquility. One thinks especially of "The Custom House," the too-long, self-justifying essay that serves as an introduction to the apparently autonomous world of *The Scarlet Letter.* In spite of the fact that it is thematically functional, its peculiar tone derives not so much from its close relationship to Hester's story as it does from an unusual mixing of aesthetic and biographical elements. Hawthorne was not unaware of the inevitable connection between the creator of Hester and the dismissed custom house official who uses his talents to mount a thinly veiled attack on his enemies. He knows the extent to which the writer of romance is dependent on "Custom-House lumber" (*CE* I, 30) in "creating the semblance of a world" (37). This he reveals when he prefaces a "tale of human frailty and sorrow" (48) with a gossipy account of some of its trivial origins.

Hawthorne is never able to forget that his fictive world is the result of an intentional act, and hence he is never able completely to transform the literary act into a literary object.[10] In spite of his nostalgia for a lost Spenserian world where natural and intentional objects are related analogically, he never confuses his fictive landscape with the natural one. Indeed the themes of failure and impotence running through all of his prefaces derive from his realization that his desire to escape from the weight of the actual is

[10] For a useful discussion of the relationship between form and intent see Paul de Man, "Form and Intent in American New Criticism," *Blindness and Insight* (New York: Oxford University Press, 1971), pp. 20–35.

doomed to failure. For him the fictive realm is best imaged as a soap bubble or delicate web, threatened on the one hand by a cynical reader and on the other by a hard reality. The image of the bubble especially pleases Hawthorne because it expresses so well the relationship between the theme of imagination and the theme of reality. The writer initially sees himself as "scattering airy spheres abroad . . . little impalpable worlds . . . with the big world depicted, in hues bright as imagination, on the nothing of their surfaces." These "brilliant fantasies" with their "pictured earth and sky scene" make the "dull atmosphere imaginative, about them" (*CE* II, 171). But these shapes are as ephemeral as they are beautiful. No more than the creation of a breath, the bubble has no fixed place nor does it possess any principle of permanence. A toy of the wind, it is homeless, dependent on the actual world for its colors and shapes and likely at any moment to be "broken by the rude contact of some actual circumstance" (*CE* I, 37).[11] Indeed it is the death of the bubble that most fascinates Hawthorne, that moment when "you thrust a finger into a soap-bubble" (*CE* III, 90), when its gleaming surface is "shattered and annihilated by contact with the Practical" (*CE* X, 454). For the death of the bubble is the death of an illusion, the image of a "mean reality thrusting itself through life's brightest illusions" (*CE* IV, 303).

The experience of the writer, then, mirrors for Hawthorne the experience of the reader who in turning the final

[11] I am indebted here to Georges Poulet's discussion of the image of the bubble in Vigny. *The Metamorphoses of the Circle*, trans. Carley Dawson and Elliott Coleman (Baltimore: The Johns Hopkins University Press, 1966), p. 163.

page of a novel finds himself once again in the ordinary world of the here and the now. Suddenly that world of fascinating adventure in which he has been so involved and which he has found so moving becomes no more than black marks on a page, and he is brought back again to his solitude.[12] As a record of a "charm that has forever vanished" (*CW* X, 164), the prefaces exist in the form of a reading by the author of his own work, and as Paul de Man, following Blanchot, has pointed out, such a self-reading by an author may be more disturbing than the experience of an ordinary reader.

Acceding to the work in its positivity, the reader can very well ignore what the author was forced to forget: that the work asserted in fact the impossibility of its own existence. However, if the writer were really reading himself, in the full interpretive sense of the term, he would necessarily remember the duplicity of his self-induced forgetfulness, and this discovery would paralyze all further attempts at creation. In that sense Blanchot's *noli me legere*, the rejection of self-interpretation, is an expression of caution, advocating a prudence without which literature might be threatened with extinction.[13]

Such a threat is always present in Hawthorne's prefaces, which function as does the mirror in which Feathertop sees the "sordid patchwork of his real composition, stript of all witchcraft" (*CE* X, 244). Hester's faded Scarlet A, the venerable Old Manse now transformed by the "sacrilegious" (*CE* X, 33) renovators, the lost "Dream-Land of his youth"

[12] See Leslie A. Fiedler's discussion of the relation of solitude and the novel in *Love and Death in the American Novel* (New York: Stein and Day, 1966), pp. 23–55.

[13] Paul de Man, "Impersonality in the Criticism of Maurice Blanchot," *Blindness and Insight*, p. 66.

(*CE* IX, 7), his "old . . . home at Brook Farm" (*CE* III, 2)—all these point to a world that resembles a "magician's cave, when the all-powerful wand is broken, and the visionary splendor vanished, and the floor strewn with fragments of scattered spells" (*CE* X, 261).

The "particular loneliness of the writer," says Blanchot, "stems from the fact that, in the work, he belongs to what always precedes the work,"[14] and Hawthorne's preoccupation with the disenchanting beginnings of his fiction seem to confirm this insight. For him, however, that loneliness of which Blanchot speaks is most poignantly expressed in the themes of homelessness and nostalgia for origins that permeate his writings.

[14] *L'Espace littéraire*, p. 14. Cited by de Man, *Blindness and Insight*, p. 65.

5

The Enchantment of Origins

If the history of thought could remain the locus of uninterrupted continuities, if it could endlessly forge connexions that no analysis could undo without abstraction, if it could weave, around everything that men say and do, obscure synthesis that anticipate for him, prepare him, and lead him endlessly towards his future, it would provide a privileged shelter for the sovereignty of consciousness. Continuous history is the indispensable correlative of the founding function of the subject: the guarantee that everything that has eluded him may be restored to him; the certainty that time will disperse nothing without restoring it in a reconstituted unity; the promise that one day the subject—in the form of historical consciousness—will once again be able to appropriate, to bring back under his sway, all those things that are kept at a distance by difference, and find in them what might be called his abode.

Michel Foucault, *The Archaeology of Knowledge*

The function of the concept of origin, as in original sin, is to summarize in one word what has not to be thought in order to be able to think what one wants to think. The concept of genesis is charged with taking charge of, and masking, a production or mutation whose recognition would threaten the vital continuity of the empiricist schema of history.

Louis Althusser, *Reading Capital*

The beginning conditions of all narrative are the possibility of consecutive explanation, and of return: the fundamental text is *The Odyssey*.

Edward Said, "Narrative: Quest for Origins and Discovery of the Mausoleum"

For Hawthorne the power of the other is not always experienced in the form of a magnetic and dangerous fascination. It is felt too in states such as loneliness and boredom which are also testimonies of the reality of the other. These are experiences Hawthorne expresses most poignantly through his use of the image of the man sick for home, an image explicitly linking the desire for the other with a nostalgia for origins. Like a number of the romantic writers he admires, Hawthorne regards himself as a "homeless man" (*LL* I, 113), an exile forced to wander "up and down, like an exorcised spirit that had been driven from its old haunts, after a mighty struggle" (*CE* III, 194). As Julian Hawthorne notes, his father, who during his married years was constantly moving from place to place, both in America and on the continent, "never found any permanent place anywhere."[1] Of course Hawthorne himself constantly

[1] "He soon wearied of any particular locality," his son continues. "A novelist would say that he inherited the roving disposition of his seafaring ancestors. Partly necessity or convenience, but partly, also, his own will, drove him from place to place; always wishing to settle down finally, but never lighting upon the fitting spot. In America he moved from place to place and longed for England. In England he traveled constantly and looked forward to France and Italy. In Paris, Rome, and Florence his affections reverted to England once more; but, having returned thither, he made it but a stepping-stone to America. Finding himself at length in Concord, he enlarged and refitted the house he had previously bought there, and tried to think that he was content to spend in it the remainder

laments his "vagrant life," his inability to "take root any-where," and insists that "it is folly for mortal man to do anything more than pitch a tent."[2] He sees himself and his family as "pilgrims and dusty wayfarers" (*CE* V, 254), "vagabonds" who live an "unsettled, shifting, vagrant life" (*EN*, 425).

I sat, last evening, as twilight came on, and thought rather sadly how many times we have changed our home, since we were married. In the first place, our three years at the Old Manse; then a brief residence at Salem, then at Boston, then two or three years at Salem again; then at Lenox, then at West Newton, and then again at Concord, where we imagined that we were fixed for life, but spent only a year. Then this further flight to England, where we expect to spend four years, and afterwards another year in Italy—during all which time we shall have no real home.   [*EN*, 23]

Even when Hawthorne returns to his home at Concord at the end of his European pilgrimage, he retains this sense of homelessness, for that residence, like all the others he has occupied, seems no more than a momentary stopping place. Consequently, he names it "The Wayside," "because I

---

of his days. No sooner had he come to this determination, however, than memories of England possessed him more and more . . . and, till near the end, cherished a secret hope that some happy freak of destiny might lead him there again" (*Hawthorne and His Wife*, I, 429).

    [2] *Letters of Hawthorne to William D. Ticknor, 1851–1864* (Newark: The Carteret Book Club, 1910), reprinted by NCR/ Microcord Editions, 1972, Letters dated Liverpool, Sept. 26th, '56; Liverpool, Jany 31st, '57; Concord, May 16th, 1861, Vol. II, 26, 39, 115. Both the root and tent metaphors are found scattered through-out the letters and Notebooks. See also *EN*, 425; *CE* V, 254–255; and *CW* X, 431, 467.

never feel as if I were more permanently located than the traveller who sits down to rest by the road which he is plodding along."[3] Hawthorne, in short, is a man whose central and repeated experience is one of exile and dispersion from a number of temporary homes; and that experience, moreover, is centrally related to his career as a writer. His fiction is, of course, filled with homeless characters who seek recognition and reconciliation. One thinks of such figures as Robin Molineux, Ethan Brand, and Giovanni Guasconti as well as most of the characters in the four major novels. Even more suggestive, however, is the fact that his prefaces are a record of a similar feeling, for it is here that the experiences of the man and the writer coincide.

The preface to the *Mosses from an Old Manse* describes the "sacrilegious" renovators who invade the sacred space of the Old Manse, that "stately edifice where we could go forth into statelier simplicity" and drive the writer and his family out "as uncertain as wandering Arabs where our tent might next be pitched" (*CE* X, 33). "The Custom House" nostalgically recalls the writer's life at the Old Manse and furnishes an account of his "unceremonious ejectment" (*CE* I, 42) from the Custom House which forces him to become a "citizen of somewhere else" (44). The preface to *The Blithedale Romance* links the book to the author's "old and affectionately remembered home, at Brook Farm" (*CE* III, 2). And, finally, the preface to *The Marble Faun* furnishes a portrait of the artist as transient. Here the author, "writing . . . in a foreign land, and after a long, long absence from [his] own" confesses that the

[3] Edward Hutchins Davidson, *Hawthorne's Last Phase* (New Haven: Yale University Press, 1949), p. 77.

novel was "sketched out during a residence of considerable length in Italy, and has been rewritten and prepared for the press in England" (*CE* IV, 2).

The prefaces, however, like the fiction are more than hopeless laments for a lost plenitude. The emphasis there on the close ties that exist between the author's personal and literary identities suggests the possibility that the fictive world can offer an alternative to a life of homeless wandering. For example, the Old Manse and the Custom House are two of a number of momentary stopping places in Hawthorne's journey through life and also important structures in his fictional world. The two prefaces in which they appear record the instability of Hawthorne's life, but they also look beyond it. If Hawthorne finds himself in a place of solitude, the Old Manse, then he inevitably moves toward a situation "in the throng of our fellow-beings" (*CE* II, 258), the Custom House; but no sooner is he settled there than he once more moves toward solitude. The very forces, however, that cause Hawthorne, the man, to feel "invaribly out of place" (*CE* II, 265) provide a generative energy for Hawthorne the writer. "The Custom House" connects the origins of *The Scarlet Letter* with Hawthorne's presence at and ejectment from the old building; and although the book is written after the author has left the oppressive public world and returned once more to a setting where the imagination is free to act, it is constructed nevertheless from "Custom-House Lumber" (*CE* I, 30). "The Custom House" then, is both an account of Hawthorne's rootless life and, at the same time, as an "entrance-hall to the magnificent edifice which he throw[s] open to [his]

guests,"[4] is the record of a homecoming. In this sense the sketch endows the familiar house-of-fiction metaphor with an important ontological dimension, for it suggests that Hawthorne has been able to find a place to rest from his "world-wanderings" (*CE* I, 11) in that house of words which he erects between himself and "this transitory world [which] is not our home" (*CE* X, 414).[5]

A similar suggestion is in the preface to *The House of the Seven Gables*, where the act of writing is again associated with the building of a house.

The Reader may perhaps choose to assign an actual locality to the imaginary events of this narrative. If permitted by the historical connection (which, though slight, was essential to his plan,) the Author would very willingly have avoided anything of this nature. Not to speak of other objections, it exposes the Romance to an inflexible and exceedingly dangerous species of criticism, by bringing his fancy-pictures almost into positive contact with the realities of the moment. It has been no part of his object, however, to describe local manners, nor in any way

---

[4] "In this latter event it appears to me that the only proper title for the book would be "The Scarlet Letter," for "The Custom House" is merely introductory,—an entrance-hall to the magnificent edifice which I throw open to my guests" (from a letter to James T. Fields cited in James T. Fields, *Yesterdays with Authors* [Boston: James R. Osgood, 1874], p. 52).

[5] As a number of critics have noticed, the theme of house-building is a recurring one in nineteenth-century American literature. See especially Richard Poirier, *A World Elsewhere* (New York: Oxford University Press, 1966), pp. 17–49, and Tony Tanner, "Notes for a Comparison between American and European Romanticism," *Journal of American Studies*, 2 (April 1968), 92–96. See also the chapter "The Search for a Home" in Roy A. Male, *Hawthorne's Tragic Vision* (New York: Norton, 1964), pp. 38–53.

to meddle with the characteristics of a community for whom he cherishes a proper respect and a natural regard. He trusts not to be considered as unpardonably offending, by laying out a street that infringes upon nobody's private rights, and appropriating a lot of land which had no visible owner, and building a house, of materials long in use for constructing castles in the air. [*CE* II, 3]

The most remarkable aspect of this passage is the suggestion that the author has been able to capture a dream all of the characters in the novel pursue unsuccessfully. Most of the characters in *The House of the Seven Gables* seek, in Phoebe's words, "for this short life of ours . . . a house and moderate garden spot of one's own" (*CE* II, 156). The novel's central tension derives from Hawthorne's realization, on the one hand, that history teaches the impossibility of man's ever being able to be at home with others and his subjective commitment, on the other, to man's undying belief in a dream house, a place that will allow man to be at home with others and with himself. Such a home will be a place of solitude and yet also spacious and open to the world, "a spot of deepest quiet, within the reach of the intensest activity" (*CE* V, 219), an area that at once can provide the proper atmosphere for the operation of the intellect and imagination and also serve as a gateway to the busy world.

No such place seems available to the characters in *The House of the Seven Gables*. The "rude hovel" the original Maule builds in the space "hewn out of the primeval forest, to be his garden ground and homestead" (7) is destroyed by social forces in the form of Colonel Pyncheon, a "prominent and powerful personage, who asserted plausible claims to the proprietorship of this, and a large adjacent tract of land, on the strength of a grant from the legislature" (7), and the house he builds, in turn, is haunted by his ghost. As a matter of fact, none of the houses in the novel are designed to provide any of their inhabitants with "home feeling." All of them are threatening in one way or another. The atmosphere of the Pyncheon house is oppressive and overwhelming as a result of the "crystallization on its walls of the human breath that has been drawn and exhaled . . . in discontent and anguish" (184); the farm to which Uncle Venner plans to retire is the "great brick house . . . the work-house most folks call it" (62); and the metaphoric edifice that describes Judge Pyncheon's public character, although spacious and beautiful from the outside, contains at its center a "pool of stagnant water, foul with many impurities, and perhaps tinged with blood" (230).

Hawthorne, however, seems to have managed to construct a house that is neither an expression of the "energy of disease" (23) which operates in society nor an indication that its architect and builder is forever separated from others. In writing the novel he seems to have participated in authentic action, involved himself in the process of building, the essence of social activity. Yet this activity does not derive its thrust from the exploitation of others. Like the pioneer, the writer of romance seems able to "lay out a street which infringes on nobody's private rights" and appropriate a "lot of land which has no visible owner."

Both "The Custom House" and the preface to *The House of the Seven Gables* seem to suggest that the writer can take fragments from the world in which he wanders an exile, subject them to the transforming powers of the imagi-

nation, and construct an abode that will allow him a sense of
freedom as well as meaningful contact with others. He will
be able to recover through his fiction a unity of being he is
unable to achieve in life. This is another romantic assumption which interests Hawthorne but which he cannot accept
unquestioningly since it implies an absolute separation of
the writer's personal and literary situations. In "The Custom
House" the author first asks that the sketch be "considered
as the POSTHUMOUS PAPERS OF A DECAPITATED
SURVEYOR . . . and if too autobiographical for a modest
person to publish in his lifetime, will be readily excused in a
gentleman who writes from beyond the grave. Peace be
with all the world! My blessings on my friends! My for-
giveness to my enemies! For I am in the realm of quiet!"
(*CE* I, 43–44). But at the same time he announces the freedom that his "figurative self" enjoys he reminds us that the
"real human being with his head safely on his shoulders . . .
had opened his long-disused writing-desk and was again a
literary man" (45). Hawthorne may be joking here, but he
is also questioning the extent to which a writer is free both
to use and to renounce the details of his personal life, an
especially important issue for him since so much of his
writing takes the form of an investigation of his personal
and cultural antecedents. Many of the early tales as well as
The Scarlet Letter reflect Hawthorne's interest in recover-
ing his national and personal origins which lie buried in the
past. Nevertheless he is always aware that the New England
past cannot offer an unequivocal point of origin beyond
which it is impossible to go. In the process of seeking out
his New England beginnings through his study of "tales,
traditions, anecdotes of famous dead people, and traits of

ancient manners" (*CE* IX, 258), he confronts only points of rupture and interruption. The Gray Champion and Old Esther Dudley are in different ways images of displacement and discontinuity. He is at once "the relic of long departed times" (*CE* IX, 14) and an image of the firstness of things beyond which an American cannot go and she an indication that "we are no longer children of the past" (302). This is the discovery too of Robin Molineux who is forced to renounce his search for his kinsman's house, to break the tie that joins two generations of his family, and to begin life unsupported by the authority of the past. Hester Prynne's radicalism is also an expression of this spirit. That radicalism, however, is tempered by Dimmesdale's conservative dependence on and commitment to the past, a commitment initially shared by his creator. As both the theory and practice make clear, Hawthorne's is an art that depends on the past even as it seeks to move beyond it. For him the ideal situation is one where the personal and historical will be preserved even as they are transcended. The Custom House will be left behind and his "old native town" will cease to be a "reality of [his] life" (*CE* I, 44), and yet he will continue to exist for future generations of Salemites through his fiction.

Unfortunately, however, like Esther Dudley and the new order of things, the real and figurative selves as well as the places they inhabit are incompatible: each can exist only at the expense of the other. From the point of view of the actual a "castle in the air is a sort of no man's land" (*CE* X, 67), an "enchanted edifice" (172) subject to the disenchanting pull of reality. Like any other imaginary structure, it is a thing of only "momentary visibility and no substance" and is destined, finally, "to be overburdened and crushed down by the first cloud-shadow that might fall upon [it]" (*CE* V, 258). Compared to "terrestrial architecture" (*CE* X, 57) the castle in the air is no more than a "heap of sunset clouds to which the magic of light and shade [has] imported the aspect of a fantastically constructed mansion" (58).

Conversely, from the point of view of the figurative self the real world is dreamlike and misty. "A dreamer may dwell so long among fantasies, that the things without him will seem as unreal as those within" (*CE* IX, 427). For the dreamer the actual becomes dematerialized, as his former life at the Custom House does for Hawthorne when he begins to write *The Scarlet Letter*, until at last it is no more than a cloud.[6] Such a metamorphosis is experienced by Septimius Felton when he gives himself up to the dream of discovering the elixir of life.

When Septimius came to look at the matter in his present mood, the thought occurred to him that he had perhaps got into such a limbo, and that Sibyl's legend, which looked so wild, might be all of a piece with his own present life; for Sibyl herself seemed an illusion, and so, most strangely, did Aunt Keziah, whom he had known all of his life, with her homely and quaint characteristics; the grim doctor, with his brandy and his German pipe, impressed him in the same way; and these, altogether, made his homely cottage by the wayside

[6] Coverdale, recalling the other-worldly schemes of his Blithedale associates, writes: "It was impossible, situated as we were, not to imbibe the idea that everything in nature and human existence was fluid, or fast becoming so; that the crust of the Earth, in many places, was broken, and its whole surface portentiously upheaving; that it was a day of crisis, and that we ourselves were in the critical vortex. Our great globe floated in the atmosphere of infinite space like an unsubstantial bubble" (*CE* III, 140–141).

seem an unsubstantial edifice, such as castles in the air are built of, and the ground he trod on unreal; and that grave, which he knew to contain the decay of a beautiful young man, but a fictitious swell formed by the fantasy of his eyes. All unreal; all illusion . . . ! In short, it was such a moment as I suppose all men feel (at least, I can answer for one), when the real scene and picture of life swims, jars, shakes, seems about to be broken up and dispersed, like the picture in a smooth pond, when we disturb its tranquil mirror by throwing in a stone; and though the scene soon settles itself, and looks as real as before, a haunting doubt keeps close at hand, as long as we live, asking, "Is it stable? Am I sure of it? Am I certainly not dreaming? See; it trembles again, ready to dissolve." [*CW* XI, 335–336]

This admirable passage expresses quite clearly the reasons the House of Fiction is unable to provide a lasting home for Hawthorne. He is drawn to the Hall of Fantasy for the same reason Septimius searches for the elixir of life. That "enchanted edifice" (*CE* X, 172) is the prefiguration or promise of a future happiness that exists at present only ideally. One visits the Hall "for the sake of spiritualizing the grossness of this actual life, and prefiguring to ourselves a state, in which the Idea shall be all in all" (*CE* X, 185). The power of fiction, in short, seems to confer the stability of sensible objects to those qualities that lie beyond the senses. The fact that the unseen can be represented is proof of its presence.[7] Unfortunately, however, such representations may also have the effect of putting into question the ontological status of the seen at the very moment they lend solidity to the unseen. The author-narrator of "Night Sketches" is driven from his writing desk by the fear that

[7] I am indebted here to Paul de Man's discussion of representation in *Blindness and Insight*, pp. 122–135.

"shadowy materials as have busied [him] throughout the day" (*CE* IX, 427) will have robbed the world of its solidity; Hepzibah Pyncheon has a similar experience when the "vivid life and reality, assumed by her emotions, made all outward occurrences unsubstantial, like the teasing phantasms of a half-conscious slumber" (*CE* II, 66); and finally, Coverdale, surrounded by "innumerable schemes of what [the world] might or ought to be" begins to "lose a sense of what kind of world it was" (*CE* III, 140).

Imaginative constructs represent the unseen, but they do it in the mode of a mirror that also reflects images of the actual. Hence an interaction between the real and fictive is established that tends to blur the distinctions between the two realms in such a way as to make the actual seem as insubstantial and fragile as the fictive. Once one has seen the actual reflected in the mirror of imagination, it in turn takes on the quality of a mirror image, having in some strange way been assimilated into the fictive and infected by the same instability one finds there. Once reality is hollowed out by this imaginary quality, it can no longer be viewed as the generative source and explanation of the fictive. The passage from *Septimius Felton* points to a breakdown in the intricate system by which things are linked to an unequivocal beginning that is the foundation of everything. Gone is the Spenserian world Hawthorne so much admired where the real and fictive realms can exist harmoniously side by side resembling one another but with each realm retaining its own singularity guaranteed it by its source, and in its place is a world of mirror images.

Obviously, in such a world the act of writing can no longer be viewed as a way of escaping the disturbances and

confusions of actuality. In the place of the security of Spenserian correspondences is the confusion of a situation where
the fictive and actual overlap and intermingle. The passage
above records an experience in the life of a fictional character, but it blends that experience with the life of the
author. Septimius, his Aunt Keziah, and the grim doctor are
fictional characters; they exist only in the novel and cannot
be encountered anywhere else. The reference to the hero's
"homely cottage by the wayside," however, as well as the
narrator's description of the instability of his own life suggest that the novel's world has not been brought into
existence out of nothing. Its source, however, is another
story, this one told to Hawthorne by Thoreau concerning
a former inhabitant of the Wayside, a man who thought he
would never die and who, therefore, "did not mean to make
his earthly abode a mere wayside seat."[8] The image of
Wayside reflected in the mirror of Thoreau's account obviously fascinates Hawthorne, and he doubles the image
when he writes a narrative based on the story. The effect
of the mirrored images, of course, is to rob Wayside of its
status as a real place even as the legendary aspects of Sep-

---

[8] "Thoreau first told me about this predecessor of mine; though,
I think he knew nothing of his character and history, nor anything
but this singular fact, that here in this simple old house, at the foot
of the hill, and so close to the Lexington road that I call it the
Wayside (partly for that, and partly because I never feel as if I
were more permanently located than the traveller who sits down to
rest by the road which he is plodding along), here dwelt, in some
long past time, this man who was resolved never to die. He, at all
events, did not mean to make of his earthly abode a mere wayside
seat, where he would sit while the sun threw his shadow a little
further on the soil; he would sit here while roses grew up and decayed; he would always be here" (Davidson, p. 77).

timius's life put into question the reality of his everyday surroundings.

It is possible, however, that this ambiguous interplay between fiction and reality that torments Hawthorne and makes it impossible for him to be at rest in either a real house or a castle in the air is not the result of some irreversible ontological disruption. His experience may follow from America's too hasty rejection of the possibility and importance of maintaining a connection with a point of origin that is the foundation and source of the present. If man could feel in touch with his beginnings, the difference between the self and the other might dissolve in the enjoyment of their common origin and the act of writing become a celebration of the "home-feeling" of pure presence. The international theme, central in *The Marble Faun* and the unfinished romances, suggests the seriousness with which Hawthorne explores this possibility. These works are permeated with a sense of nostalgia for lost origins and natural innocence. In *The Marble Faun*, for example, American artists, shivering "at the remembrance of their lonely studios in the unsympathizing cities of their native lands" (*CE* IV, 132), initially believe that in Rome they have found "their ideal home," that as a result of breathing its "enchanted air" they need no longer remain "isolated strangers" (132). To them Rome seems "more familiar, more intimately [their] home, than even the spot where [they] were born" (326). This sense of "home-feeling" presumably derives from the fact that in the Old World, unlike the New, man has not been so quick to "cast off the whole tissue of ancient custom, like a tattered garment" (*CE* X, 180). Here, surrounded by a "threefold antiquity" (*CE* IV, 6) and provided with an elaborate set of ceremonies of presence to mediate between himself and others, he seems almost able to reach back across the distance separating him from his lost origins.

Nevertheless, as we have seen, *The Marble Faun* is a novel conceived and written in exile. Moreover, it is a book of precipices and chasms, of perspectives and distances. The characters are separated one from the other by a "voiceless gulf" (13); each finds himself an "alien in the world," with a "wholly unsympathetic medium betwixt himself and those whom he yearns to meet" (92). Other people are "within . . . view" and yet, "beyond . . . reach" (66), enveloped by a "strange distance and unapproachableness" (89). Nor do the elaborate gardens and ceremonial carnivals successfully mediate between man and nature and man and other men. In the same way the complicated rituals of the Catholic Church are unable to bridge the distance that separates man from the lost state of plenitude. Like the carnival, the church is "traditionary not actual" (436) and is "alive this present year, only because it has existed through centuries gone by" (436). It stands, therefore, as another manifestation of the theme of absence, for it has lost the "dignity and holiness of its origins" (345). In the place of "general medicaments" (345) for the sick soul, it can offer only "cordials" (344) and "sedatives" (345). Saint Peter's cathedral contains no "cure . . . for a sick soul, but it would make an admirable atmospheric hospital for sick bodies" (360). This tendency to reduce the spiritual to the physical, moreover, leads to an even more deceptive reduction, the transformation of a theocentric relationship into an interpersonal one.[9]

[9] I am indebted here to Paul de Man's discussion of a similar re-

Hilda saw peasants, citizens, soldiers, nobles, women with bare heads, ladies in their silks, entering the churches, individually, kneeling for moments, or for hours, and directing their inaudible devotions to the shrine of some Saint of their choice. In his hallowed person, they felt themselves possessed of an own friend in Heaven. They were too humble to approach the Deity directly. Conscious of their unworthiness, they asked the mediation of their sympathizing patron, who, on the score of his ancient martyrdom, and after many ages of celestial life, might venture to talk with the Divine Presence almost as friend with friend. [346–347]

The sympathy generated by such a relationship is as much a mystification as that produced by the sylvan dance and the carnival. Donatello receives the "bronze Pontiff's benediction" (315), as he seems by his "look and gesture" (324) to approve of the young Italian's union with Miriam, only to be separated from her and imprisoned by the priestly rulers of Rome. Similarly, Hilda, seeking relief from her troubled conscience, receives the benediction of the old priest who hears her confession and later becomes a prisoner in the convent of the Sacré Coeur, watched over by that same priest. The forms of the church, in other words, no longer derive authority from something beyond them; its "mighty machinery" (345) is managed by human engineers, and it operates in a world where things have lost their analogical sense. High and low no longer indicate the direction of salvation and damnation; the Palazzo de Torre does not sink into the earth when the lamp of the Virgin is extinguished, as a priest had insisted that it would. Hilda's

---

duction in Coleridge's thought. See his "The Rhetoric of Temporality" in *Interpretation: Theory and Practice*, ed. Charles Singleton (Baltimore: The Johns Hopkins University Press, 1968), p. 182.

tower is no more symbolic than Donatello's. One is a "dove-cote" (54), the other, an "owl-tower" (252), one a shrine of the Virgin, the other a "strong-hold of times long past" (215), but both are "square," "lofty," and "massive" (51, 214); and Kenyon, standing in one tower, is reminded of the other "turret that ascended into the sky of the summer afternoon" (264). The point, of course, is that neither Hilda's tower with the shrine and doves nor Donatello's with the crucifix and death's head allows either of the young people to avoid sin or adequately to deal with its consequences. Both structures mock man's "feeble efforts to soar upward" (256), for they imply the absence of any kind of spacial hierarchy. Donatello finds relief only when he leaves his ancestral tower for the crowded market place of Perugia, and Hilda comes "down from her old tower, to be herself enshrined and worshipped as a household Saint, in the light of her husband's fireside" (461).

The experiences of the characters in *The Marble Faun* put into question the assumption that a devotion to the past will lead finally to a discovery of an unequivocal beginning point and with it a sense of "home-feeling." At the end of the novel Hilda and Kenyon renounce the towers, ruins, and ceremonies of the Old World, which in seeking to overcome absence only succeed in signifying it, and turn toward the New World which they now regard as a place of "human promise" (461). Their solution, however, cannot work for the romancer. He must remain in exile because "romance and poetry . . . need ruin to make them grow" (3). In other words there is a tension in the novel between the characters' disenchanted view of the Old World and the novelist's own realization that fiction is based on an idea

of continuous history and is always in an important sense
a quest for a native land or an original home. This tension
is present in the distance that separates the narrator from his
characters and in the "lack of continuousness and dependence in [the] narrative" (*CE* IV, 93). Its full implications,
however, are explored not in *The Marble Faun* but in the
Ancestral Home fragments that occupy Hawthorne's attention during the last sad years of his life. Here the search of
a character for his beginnings is explicitly linked to the
genesis of romance; the house of fiction is equated with the
Ancestral Home.

> If you know anything of me, you know how I sprang out of
> mystery, akin to none, a thing concocted out of the elements,
> without visible agency—how, all through my boyhood, I was
> alone; how I grew up without a root, yet continually longing
> for one—longing to be connected with somebody—and never
> feeling myself so. . . . I have tried to keep down this yearning,
> to stifle it, annihilate it, with making a position for myself, with
> being my own past; but I cannot overcome this natural horror
> of being a creature floating in the air, attached to nothing; ever
> this feeling that there is no reality in the life and fortunes, good
> or bad, of a being so unconnected. There is not even a grave,
> not a heap of dry bones, not a pinch of dust, with which I
> can claim connection. [*DGS*, 145]

This passage expresses clearly the fundamental experience
that lies behind the sense of homelessness that torments
Hawthorne and his characters. The orphan whose origins
are lost in "impenetrable obscurity" (*DGS*, 71) and who is
burdened by the feeling that he was born "out of darkness
and mystery, out of nothingness, out of a kingdom of
shadows; out of dust, clay, impure mud" (213) is the perfect expression of the fact that an other has priority over the

self. The feeling of loneliness the passage expresses derives from the experience of the other but the experience of the other as now absent. What the orphan seeks, however, is not simply recognition by a community. He understands that an American can be born an "almshouse child" (54) and still play an important and dignified role in the eyes of others. But he is not satisfied when he has achieved status in the community by making himself an economic and political success. He defines himself and imposes that definition on others, but these positive acts are unable to relieve his "dreary sense of solitude" (55). The others who surround him are mere physical presences, or worse, rivals who resist his efforts to find some positive ground for his identity. What he demands is an other to whom he is "connected by blood" (55), some other in whom he can see himself. Such a presence would mean that he would no longer have to define himself negatively through an experience of what he is not but would instead enjoy the feeling of being at home in a world where he truly belongs.

The ideal of an Ancestral Home describes a world where such a full experience of presence is possible. Once the orphan comes to believe that he is the descendant of the lost heir of an Old English family his feelings of alienation and longing disappear and are supplanted by a new sense of solidity and continuity in his life. In the place of the horrible feeling that he is a "creature floating in the air" is the reassuring sense that his personal identity is continuous with that of his ancestors.

The thought thrilled his bosom, that this was his home;—the home of the wild western wanderer, who had gone away centuries ago, and encountered strange chances, and almost for-

gotten his origin, but still kept a clue to bring him back, and
had now come back and found all the original emotions safe
within him. It even seemed to him, that by his kindred with
those who had gone before—by the line of sensitive blood linking him with that first emigrant, he could remember all those
objects,—that tree, hardly more venerable now than then; that
clock-tower, still marking the elapsing time; that spire of the
old church raising itself beyond. He spread out his arms in a
kind of rapture, and exclaimed:—

"Oh home, my home, my forefathers' home! I have come
back to thee! The Wanderer has come back." [*DGS*, 146][10]

What the young American experiences here is not merely a
memory perpetuated by a ruin or a tombstone. His kindred
are in some way alive in him, and he feels their presence as a
confirmation of his own identity. The presence of that "line
of sensitive blood" unlocks a family memory that confirms
genealogical continuity in the same way that personal
memory preserves the sense of a continuous self. Hence he
completes his ancestor's journey, senses his emotions, sees
with his eyes: "it seemed more and more to him as if he
were the very individual—the self-same one throughout the
whole—who had done, seen, suffered, all these long toils and
vicissitudes, and were now come back to rest" (*CW* XI,
510). It is the Ancestral Home that generates these reassuring feelings of continuity, for, unlike the Wayside and

[10] An interesting parallel passage occurs in *The Ancestral Footstep:* "He was now at home; yes, he had found his home, and was
sheltered at last under the ancestral roof after all those long, long
wanderings,—after the little log-built hut of the early settlement,
after the straight roof of the American house, after all the many
roofs of two hundred years, here he was at last under the one
which he had left, on that fatal night, when the Bloody Footstep
was so mysteriously impressed on the threshold" (*CW* XI, 510).

other "poor tents of a day, inns of a night, where nothing [is] certain, save that the family of him who built it would not dwell here, even if he himself should have the bliss to die under the roof" (*DGS*, 97), this dwelling can provide the inhabitant with a sense of "home feeling" (52).

And so he lay in a kind of peaceful luxury, not seeking any longer to put his finger to the evolution of his own fate. It was sweet to resign himself, for the first time since he was a child, to have nothing to do with himself; to accept everything; not even to imagine forward, but to lie and let half-defined thoughts succeed one another through his mind, and to look at the devices on the walls through half-shut eyes. . . . This state was not merely the result of bodily weakness, but also it was the rest which a mind that had known hard toil and exertion . . . was now taking in this unlooked for situation. [64]

Finding himself in a house where "his every part and peculiarity . . . at once fitted into its nooks and crannies" (163), the hero for the first time enjoys the luxury of feeling that his life does not have to be sustained by his own creative efforts. Here he does not have "to put his finger to the evolution of his own fate" (64) by willing his future, because he inhabits a world that offers positive assurances of his existence. Rather than having willfully to assert an identity in the face of experiences of what he is not, he feels secure enough "to wait patiently until a change should come without any agency of his own" (64). There is no need to take a defensive posture in order to prevent the transformation of inner shadows into substance, for all signs of otherness here offer confirmation of one's own identity. Even the ghosts haunt the family hearth and hall not by "diffusing dim ghostly terrors, and repulsive shrinkings, and death in life; but in warm, genial attributes, making this life now passing more dense as it were, by adding all the substance of their own to it" (97).

This experience, moreover, is not merely a local or personal one. The hero's voyage and discovery imply that the history of mankind like that of his family is a totality, that nothing is ever really lost. "He sought his ancient home as if he had found his way into Paradise and were there endeavoring to trace out the sight [site] of Eve's bridal bower, the birthplace of the human race and its glorious possibilities of happiness and high performance" (*CW* XI, 437). The young man's discovery of his origins, in other words, is a prefiguration of man's discovery of the fount of life itself and with that discovery the end of the necessity for wandering. The wandering American's return at last to his old home is the image for a recovered plenitude which completes the circle of human history.[11]

The Ancestral Home, then, may be seen as a "castle in the air,—the shadowy threshold of which should assume substance enough to bear his foot, its thin fantastic walls actually protect him from sun and rain, its hall echo with footsteps, its hearth warm him" (*DGS*, 143). As a "visionary" construct it embodies man's dreams and desires, and, at the same time, as a structure of "real substance of ancient, ivy-grown, hewn stone" (261) it is truly inhabitable. There is, in short, a happy coincidence of shadow and substance in the form of an incarnation that does not disenchant. Consequently, like the castle of the Duke and Duchess in Book II of *Don*

---

[11] For a suggestive discussion of the romantic theme of the circuitous journey, see M. H. Abrams, *Natural Supernaturalism* (New York: Norton, 1971), pp. 141–324.

Quixote, it seems a place that successfully bridges the gap between imagination and perception.

Life as it is lived at such places, however, can be disturbing to those who value their freedom. Like the wandering Quixote when he is treated for the first time as a true knight-errant, the young American begins to be troubled by a feeling that he is "enthralled" by a "witchcraft, and undefinable spell, a something that he could not define" (172). Although he is at one with his surroundings for the first time in his life, he senses that his situation may be that of a "patient" in a "delirium, or waking dream" (60) who enters another world at the expense of having left the actual one behind.

After strife, anxiety, great mental exertion, and excitement of various kinds, which had harassed him ever since he grew to be a man, had come this opportunity of perfect rest; this dream in the midst of which he lay, while its magic boundaries involved him, and kept far the contact of actual life, so that its sounds and tumults seemed remote; its cares could not fret him, its ambitions, objects good or evil, were shut out from him; the electric wires, that connected him with the battery of life, were broken for the time, and he did not feel the unquiet influence that kept everybody else in galvanic action. [*DGS*, 284]

Because he has known only the "hard, hot, practical life of America" (26), the young wanderer, sheltered by the old English mansion, feels that he is in a "land of enchantment, where [he] can get hold of nothing that lends [him] firm support" (147). Life is "like a romance" (147), filled with a "delicious, thrilling uncertainty between reality and fancy" (143). Indeed, once he commits himself to this dream-house-made-real, his destiny is no longer in his own hands, but follows the pattern of a gothic romance. As he explores the family mansion, seeking out its dark corners and secret rooms, he finds himself more and more bound by its "dreary ancestral hall, its mouldy dignity, its life of the past" (172). And there are more threatening "delusions, snares, pitfalls" (155) in the figure of the romantic villain, Lord Brathwaite, who drugs the hero and imprisons him in a secret room at the center of the house.

This adventure, like Hilda's and Kenyon's experiences in Rome, turns the wanderer's thoughts back to America. In *The Ancestral Footstep* the hero resists the "deep yearning for that sense of long, long rest in an age-consecrated home, which he had felt so deeply to be the happy lot of Englishmen" as a feeling "not belonging to his country, nor to the age, nor any longer possible" (*CW* XI, 518). Consequently he foregoes his claims to the estate and commits himself to the "life of an American, with its lofty possibilities for himself and his race" (517).

In *Dr. Grimshaw's Secret*, however, there is no choice to make. The hero's quest turns out to have been an empty one. He "prove[s] to have no ancestry," to be an "American son of nobody" (*DGS*, 122). Being "deprived of all kindred" it seems, is the "truly American condition" (128) and one which brings with it certain clear advantages. To begin with, such a position frees one from the forces of "birth and blood which have been so powerful in past ages" (122) and leaves one free to shape his own destiny. From this point of view the orphan is regarded as lucky to have escaped the limiting and defining boundaries of an inherited identity. Because his parental and social origins are unknown, he has "all the world, all possibilities to choose his ancestry from . . . so that he may, in fancy, trace his origin to the King's palace, if he likes" (54). This freedom, moreover, leads to the possibility of new definitions of society and social roles. Once the hero has ended his quest for his origins (which are a prefiguration of Eve's bridal bower, the birthplace of the human race) he and his beloved are free to "become the Adam and Eve of a new epoch, and the fitting missionaries of a new social faith" (*CW* XI, 490). Or, to put the point another way, once they as Americans have renounced the idea of an Ancestral Home, they develop the admirable "faculty for making [themselves] at home anywhere" (*DGS*, 163).

As Hawthorne recognizes, however, such a conclusion is not one "satisfactory to the natural yearnings of novel readers" (*CW* XI, 44); for they will expect the pattern one finds in such narratives as *Tom Jones* and *Great Expectations* which end with the discovery of either a real or surrogate father for the hero. The thrust of Hawthorne's narrative, however, is not to make the birth of his hero intelligible in traditional terms but to demystify the assumption that a fixed origin is necessary to orient and organize a life. The reader initially is offered a traditional plot that brings "forward the infant heir out of obscurity, and [makes] plain the links, the filaments, which [connect] that feeble childish life, in a far country, with the great tide of noble life, embracing great strands of kindred, which . . . come down like a chain from antiquity, in old England" (*DGS*, 215). This is a plot based on a theory of continuous history and implies that the thread of any individual life is inescapably woven into the fabric of the past in such a way that nothing is ever really lost. The hero arrives in

England expecting to find a "thread, to which the thread he had so long held in his hand might seem ready to join on" (*CW* XI, 442). What he discovers, however, is that the continuity he experiences is the result of a "wild web of madness" spun by the spidery old Doctor who has raised him: "The Doctor must have a great agency in these doings, both of the Pensioner and Etheridge, making tissues of cobweb out of men's life-threads; he must have the air, in the Romance, of a sort of magician, without being called so. . . . Hold on to this. A dark, subtle manager, for the love of managing, like a spider sitting in the center of his web which stretches far to east and west" (*DGS*, 122).

It is the old Doctor who first arouses the hero's interest in his unknown origins and who forges the connection that leads the young man to England and to the privileged shelter of the ancestral home. " 'Let me alone,' " he says to his young charge, " 'and I shall spin out the web that shall link you with that race' " (*DGS*, 215). Such activity, of course, associates the old Doctor with the romancer, who spins similar webs, and, indeed, the language Hawthorne uses in describing his difficulties with the Old Home fragments makes the connection explicit: "It is a snarled skein, truly; but I half fancy there is a way to unravel the threads, by dint of breaking one or two" (123), he writes to himself, only later to add the desperate conclusion, "It is all an entanglement" (278).

This startling association of the novelist with the revenge-driven old Doctor as well as the description of the Ancestral Home as a castle in the air that generates the atmosphere of romance is evidence that the Old Home fragments are a subversive critique of the entire enterprise of the romancer.

As we have seen, Hawthorne looks to romance as a way to span the distance between the self and the other by mediating those polarities that constitute for him the matrix of human relationships. He hopes that in a "neutral territory" the tensions between shadow and substance, solitude and involvement, reading (fascination) and interpretation, and love and desire will be relieved if not resolved. Finally, however, the uneasiness and suspicion with which he has always regarded the act of writing overwhelm these dreams. At last he comes to see that fiction is no more than a symptom of the condition it at once laments and seeks to overcome. The dialectic of enchantment and disenchantment, possession and dispossession that governs the forms of the relationship of the self and the other is seen to be the result of a myth of origin which posits an original unity lost to the lonely wanderer now but destined to be regained at some point in the future. Once that myth is identified and rejected the idea of romance loses its validity. There is no longer a need to mediate between the self and the other because that relationship, presumably, will no longer be thought of in terms of a set of opposites which in some way must be neutralized. Whatever form human relationships take in the New World, they will not be controlled by that old dream of a reunion on native ground, a dream which the house of fiction metaphor with its suggestions of reunification through mediation embodies and perpetuates.

Replacing that figure is the metaphor of the web of fiction that demystifies the myth of origins by suggesting the extent to which narrative or story is the product of will and desire rather than a reconstruction of tradition or a representation of qualities that lie beyond the senses. The spider's web is a sort of home too but one whose materials and structure have only an inner source. Its perfect design and symmetry, a series of circumferences linked by sensitive strands to a structuring and originating center, does not represent some universal order but has been designed to meet the dark purposes of the creature that has produced it. The original ground the hero of the Ancestral Home fragments seeks is the creation of a "dark, subtle manager" and is the center of the web that entangles him. That same ground, moreover, is the force that makes his life a story by furnishing it with unity and continuity, motive and significance. Once the ground is gone so is the need for and the possibility of story. Life in the New World is based on difference and discontinuity, on acting rather than on telling. In the end Hawthorne rejects the "seductions" of origins that do not "act upon" the "higher impulses of our nature": "I should think ill of the American who, for any causes of ambition,—any hope of wealth or rank—or even for the sake of those old, delightful ideas of the past, the associations of ancestry, the loveliness of an age-long home—the old poetry and romance that haunt these ancient villages and estates of England—would give up the chance of acting upon the unmoulded future of America" (*CW* XI, 505). Like Scott's Waverley, after the skirmish at Clifton, the hero of the Ancestral Home fragments comes to recognize that the romance of his life has ended and that its real history has commenced. For Hawthorne, however, that experience records the end rather than the beginning of a writing career, for it signifies the end of story as he understands it.

Works Cited

Abrams, M. H. *Natural Supernaturalism.* New York: W. W. Norton, 1971.

Allott, Miriam. *Novelists on the Novel.* New York: Columbia University Press, 1966.

Althusser, Louis. *Reading Capital.* Trans. Ben Brewster. New York: Pantheon Books, 1970.

Barthes, Roland. *Critical Essays.* Trans. Richard Howard. Evanston, Ill.: Northwestern University Press, 1972.

Bersani, Leo. *Balzac to Beckett: Center and Circumference in French Fiction.* New York: Oxford University Press, 1970.

Brown, Homer O. "The Displaced Self in the Novels of Daniel Defoe." *English Literary History,* 38 (December 1971), 562–590.

Conway, Moncure D. *Life of Nathaniel Hawthorne.* London: Walter Scott Ltd., 1895.

Cowley, Malcolm, ed. *The Portable Hawthorne.* New York: Viking Press, 1969.

Davidson, Edward. *Hawthorne's Last Phase.* New Haven: Yale University Press, 1949.

Feidelson, Charles. "*The Scarlet Letter.*" Ed. Roy Harvey Pearce, *Hawthorne Centenary Essays* (Columbus: Ohio State University Press, 1964), pp. 31–77.

——. *Symbolism and American Literature.* Chicago: University of Chicago Press, 1953.

Fenichel, Otto. *The Collected Papers of Otto Fenichel.* New York: W. W. Norton, 1953.

Fiedler, Leslie. *Love and Death in the American Novel.* New York: Stein and Day, 1966.

Fields, James T. *Yesterdays with Authors.* Boston: James R. Osgood, 1874.

Foucault, Michel. *The Archaeology of Knowledge*. Trans. A. M. Sheridan Smith. New York: Pantheon Books, 1972.

——. *The Birth of the Clinic*. Trans. A. M. Sheridan Smith. New York: Pantheon Books, 1973.

Freccero, John. "Zeno's Last Cigarette." *Modern Language Notes*, 77 (1962), 3–23.

Hartman, Geoffrey. *Beyond Formalism*. New Haven: Yale University Press, 1970.

Hawthorne, Julian. *Hawthorne and His Wife*. 2 vols. Cambridge: James R. Osgood, 1884.

Hawthorne, Nathaniel. *The Centenary Edition of the Works of Nathaniel Hawthorne*. Eds. William Charvat, Roy Harvey Pearce, and Claude Simpson. Columbus: Ohio State University Press, 1962–.

The Scarlet Letter, vol. I, 1962.

The House of the Seven Gables, vol. II, 1965.

The Blithedale Romance, vol. III, 1964.

The Marble Faun, vol. IV, 1968.

Our Old Home, vol. V, 1970.

The American Notebooks, vol. VIII, 1972.

Twice-told Tales, vol. IX, 1974.

Mosses from an Old Manse, vol. X, 1974.

——. *The Complete Works of Nathaniel Hawthorne*. 12 vols. Cambridge: Houghton, Mifflin, 1882.

The Snow Image and Other Twice-Told Tales, vol. III.

A Wonder-Book, Tanglewood Tales, and *Grandfather's Chair*, vol. IV.

French and Italian Note-Books, vol. X.

The Dolliver Romance and *Septimius Felton*, vol. XI.

Tales, Sketches, and *Other Papers*, vol. XII.

——. *Doctor Grimshaw's Secret*. Ed. Edward H. Davidson. Cambridge: Harvard University Press, 1954.

——. *The English Notebooks*. Ed. Randall Stewart. New York: Modern Language Association, 1941. Reprinted, New York: Russell & Russell, 1962.

——. *Letters of Hawthorne to William D. Ticknor, 1851–1864*.

Newark: The Carteret Book Club, 1910. Reprinted with Foreword by C. E. Frazer Clark. Washington: NCR/Microcard Editions, 1972.

——. *The Love Letters of Nathaniel Hawthorne 1839–1863.* 2 vols. Chicago: The Society of the Dofobs, 1907. Reprinted in one vol., Foreword by C. E. Frazer Clark. Washington: NCR/Microcard Editions, 1972.

James, Henry. *Hawthorne.* Garden City: Doubleday, n.d.

Jonas, Hans. *The Phenomenon of Life.* New York: Dell, 1966.

Laing, R. D. *Self and Others.* New York: Pantheon Books, 1969.

Lathrop, Rose Hawthorne. *Memories of Hawthorne.* Boston: Houghton, Mifflin, 1897.

Macksey, Richard, and Eugenio Donato, eds. *The Languages of Criticism and the Sciences of Man.* Baltimore: The Johns Hopkins University Press, 1970.

Male, Roy. *Hawthorne's Tragic Vision.* New York: W. W. Norton, 1964.

Man, Paul de. *Blindness and Insight.* New York: Oxford University Press, 1971.

——. "The Rhetoric of Temporality." Ed. Charles Singleton, *Interpretation: Theory and Practice* (Baltimore: The Johns Hopkins University Press, 1968), pp. 173–209.

Metcalf, Eleanor Melville. *Herman Melville: Cycle and Epicycle.* Cambridge: Harvard University Press, 1953.

Miller, J. Hillis. *The Disappearance of God.* Cambridge: Harvard University Press, 1963.

——. *The Form of Victorian Fiction.* Notre Dame: University of Notre Dame Press, 1968.

Ortega y Gasset, José. *Meditations on Quixote.* Trans. Evelyn Rugg and Diego Marin. New York: W. W. Norton, 1961.

——. *On Love.* Trans. Toby Talbot. Cleveland: World, 1957.

——. *What is Philosophy?* Trans. Mildred Adams. New York: W. W. Norton, 1960.

Poirier, Richard. *A World Elsewhere.* New York: Oxford University Press, 1966.

Poulet, Georges. *The Metamorphoses of the Circle.* Trans.

Carley Dawson and Elliott Coleman. Baltimore: The Johns Hopkins University Press, 1966.

——. "Poulet on Poulet: The Self and the Other in Critical Consciousness." *Diacritics*, 2 (Spring 1972), 46–50.

Ricoeur, Paul. *Freud and Philosophy*. Trans. Denis Savage. New Haven: Yale University Press, 1970.

Said, Edward W. "Molestation and Authority in Narrative Fiction." Ed. J. Hillis Miller, *Aspects of Narrative: Selected Papers from the English Institute* (New York: Columbia University Press), pp. 47–68.

——. "Narrative: Quest for Origins and Discovery of the Mausoleum." *Salmagundi* (Spring 1970), 63–75.

Sartre, Jean Paul. *Being and Nothingness*. Trans. Hazel Z. Barnes. New York: Citadel Press, 1971.

Starobinski, Jean. *The Invention of Liberty 1700–1789*. Trans. Bernard C. Swift. Geneva: Skira, 1964.

——. "Truth in Masquerade." Ed. Victor Brombert, *Stendhal: A Collection of Critical Essays* (Englewood Cliffs: Prentice-Hall, 1962), pp. 114–126.

Tanner, Tony. "Notes for a Comparison between American and European Romanticism." *Journal of American Studies*, 2 (April 1968), 92–96.

Turner, Arlin. "Introduction." Nathaniel Hawthorne, *The Blithedale Romance*. New York: W. W. Norton, 1958.

Index

NATHANIEL HAWTHORNE

Designed by R. E. Rosenbaum.
Composed by York Composition Company, Inc.,
in 11 point linotype Janson, 3 points leaded,
with display lines in Weiss.
Printed letterpress from type by York Composition Co.
on Warren's Olde Style Wove, 60 pound basis.
Bound by John H. Dekker & Sons, Inc.
in Holliston book cloth
and stamped in All Purpose foil.

Library of Congress Cataloging in Publication Data
(For library cataloging purposes only)

Dryden, Edgar A.
  Nathaniel Hawthorne.: the poetics of enchantment.

  Bibliography: p.
  Includes index.
  1. Hawthorne, Nathaniel, 1804–1864—Criticism and interpretation.
PS1888.D7   813'.3   76–28010
ISBN 0–8014–1028–2